Pope's Essay On Criticism

John Churton Collins

POPE'S ESSAY ON CRITICISM

POPE'S

ESSAY ON CRITICISM

EDITED, WITH INTRODUCTION AND NOTES

BY

JOHN CHURTON COLLINS, M.A.

London

MACMILLAN AND CO., LIMITED

NEW YORK: THE MACMILLAN COMPANY

1896

GLASGOW: PRINTED AT THE UNIVERSITY PRESS
BY ROBERT MACLEHOSE AND CO.

PREFACE.

THE task of editing any portion of Pope's writings has been so much lightened by the labours of four generations of commentators that there is now very little room for original research, or for any important additions either in the way of commentary or illustration. I have had before me the editions of Warburton, Warton, Bowles, Roscoe, Elwin, and Courthope, the notes of Wakefield, Conington's interesting essay, and I am indebted to them all, but especially to Mr. Elwin's notes and to Mr. Courthope's excellent Life of Pope. As this edition is designed mainly for the use of students, both in England and in the Colonies, the notes are very copious, but I have endeavoured to make them as succinct and relevant as I could. I have, I hope, left no passage or even word, likely to present any difficulty, unexplained. It has been necessary to quote somewhat freely from ancient classical authors, but where quotations have been given they have always been translated. It seems a great pity that instruction in the principles of criticism should be so generally neglected, both in our schools and in our colleges, and so little encouraged by those who prescribe the subjects of study in our higher government examinations. The proper place of the *Essay on Criticism* is no doubt beside Horace's *Ars Poetica*, and it is better adapted for classical than for non-classical students, but to non-classical students it would be perfectly intelligible, and the study of it could not fail to be of benefit to them in more ways than one.

CONTENTS.

MEMOIR OF POPE.

ALEXANDER POPE, the Boileau of English Literature, and the most illustrious poet of the Critical School, was born in Lombard Street, London, on the 21st of May, 1688—a memorable year, for it was the year of the Revolution. His father was a linen-draper, but, according to Pope, belonged to a gentle family, the head of which was the Earl of Downe. This connection, however, with the family of that nobleman appears to have been a bold fiction devised by Pope to refute the taunt, so often levelled at him by the Dunces and others, that he was of humble and obscure descent. It has been conjectured by Joseph Hunter that the poet's grandfather was one Alexander Pope, Rector of Thruxton, in Hampshire, who died in 1645. His mother, who was his father's second wife, was the daughter of William Turner, Esq., of York, one of whose brothers died in the service of Charles I. To all this Pope refers in his *Epistle to Dr. Arbuthnot* or *Prologue to the Satires*, where, speaking of his descent, he says:

> "Of gentle blood (part shed in honour's cause,
> While yet in Britain honour had applause,)
> Each parent sprung."

To both his parents he was tenderly attached. He has drawn his father's character in the *Epistle to Dr. Arbuthnot*, and to his mother there is a very touching reference in the same poem,[1] and again in the *Essay on Man*.[2] Both his parents were Roman Catholics, and though Pope's religious ideas in his mature years probably differed little from those of his friend Bolingbroke, he adhered formally to that creed all his life. He belonged, therefore, to a proscribed sect: the public schools were closed against him, so also were the universities, and all the instruction he could get he could get only from the Catholic seminaries or from private teachers. An aunt taught him his letters; writing he taught himself by copying printed books. At eight years of age he received some instruction in Latin and Greek from one Bannister, a priest. In the following year he was sent to a Roman Catholic seminary at Twyford, near Winchester, where, according to his own account, he unlearnt whatever he had gained from his first tutor. Then one Deane, who had been a Fellow of University College, Oxford, and who had recently set up a school at Hyde Park Corner, took him in hand. But he learnt very little

[1] 394-405:

"Me, let the tender office long engage
To rock the cradle of reposing age;
With lenient arts extend a mother's breath,
Make languor smile, and smoothe the bed of death,
Explore the thought, explain the asking eye,
And keep awhile one parent from the sky."

[2] *Epistle* IV., 109-10:

"Or why so long (in life if long can be)
Lent Heav'n a parent to the poor and me."

from Deane. After he had left Deane's school another priest gave him lessons for a few months; and "this," he says, "was all the teaching I ever had, and, God knows, it extended a very little way." He was now in his thirteenth year, and from that time he educated himself.

Meanwhile his father had retired from business, and had taken a house at Binfield, near Wokingham, in Berkshire, "a choice," says Mr. Courthope, "no doubt determined by the fact that numerous Roman Catholic families were settled in or near Windsor Forest." Here, little more than a child though he was, Pope's serious life commenced. He was already ambitious to become a poet. He wrote a tragedy, an epic poem, with panegyrics on all the princes in Europe, and "thought himself the greatest genius that ever was." His idol and model was Dryden, and so anxious was he to see his master, that he persuaded some friends to take him to Will's Coffee House that he might be able to say, as oftentimes afterwards he did say, "*Virgilium vidi.*" The boy's studies were serious, but desultory. He read Greek, Latin, Italian, and French; he read very widely in English, being particularly attracted by Spenser, Waller, Cowley, and the poets of the metaphysical and critical schools. Appreciation and sympathy led to imitation, and to this period, no doubt, belong the "Studies," which appeared afterwards in revised forms in his works, that is, the translations from Ovid and Statius, the adaptations of Chaucer, and with one exception the imitations of the chief English poets. His extraordinary precocity is illustrated by the *Ode to Solitude,* written, he tells us, at about twelve years old, which he professes to have published in the form in which it originally appeared. While he was thus engaged he made several friends, and among them Sir William Trumbull, who had been ambassador at Constantinople, a Lord of the Treasury and Secretary of State, and who had recently settled at Easthampstead Park. At Trumbull's house he may have met the eminent comic dramatist, William Wycherley, then a man advanced in years, and William Walsh, one of the most distinguished critics of that time. In any case, they were among the earliest of his friends. To Walsh Pope owed a piece of advice which may be said to have furnished him with the ideal which ever afterwards guided him in his artistic life. "He used to encourage me much, and used to tell me there was one way left of excelling; for though we had several great poets, we never had any one great poet that was *correct*, and he desired me to make that my study and aim." And "correctness," not in the sense in which Macaulay and De Quincey have affected to understand the term, but in the sense in which Walsh and Pope understand it, became his study and aim from that moment till the moment when death brushed the pen from his hands; and this "correctness" is one of his distinguishing characteristics.

The works which first brought Pope into notice were the *Pastorals*. As his statements can seldom be depended upon, it is impossible to say exactly when the *Pastorals* were written; but it seems clear that one or more of them must have been written before he was eighteen. They were published in Tonson's *Sixth Mis-*

cellany, on the 2nd of May, 1709. From this moment he became famous. "It is no flattery at all to say," rapturously wrote Walsh, "that Virgil had written nothing so good at his age." The *Pastorals* represent only a small portion of the work which Pope had produced, and which was still in manuscript, and *sub limâ* between 1700 and 1709. His intense application had weakened and impaired his physical constitution, delicate from his birth, and sown the seeds of the various maladies which were to make his life, as he afterwards pathetically described it, "a long disease." As a child of ten he was, we are told, plump and healthy, neither a dwarf nor deformed; but as he advanced into his teens, he became ricketty and sickly, he ceased to grow, his figure got distorted—his back was so weak that he had to be laced up in stiff canvas stays to prevent collapse; he could neither dress nor undress himself without assistance. Tortured with dyspepsia, and racked with excruciating headaches, he never, in mature life, knew the sensation of health. But his astonishing nervous energy, vitality, and mental vigour completely triumphed over physical ailments and depression; and in the race for fame he was not even handicapped, as the result showed, by impediments which would have been fatal to most men.

As early as 1707, perhaps earlier, he had been hard at work on the *Essay on Criticism*, which appeared anonymously in May, 1711. If any proof were needed of Pope's unwearied diligence and assiduity as a student, it would be afforded by this poem, which is little more than a cento of what is best in Greek, Latin, Italian, French, and English criticism. In the

Essay on Criticism is sounded the first note of the war with the Dunces: the attack on Dennis may be said to initiate the controversies in which Pope was destined to waste so much precious time. The *Essay on Criticism* was succeeded by the *Messiah* and *Windsor Forest*, the first of which was published in the *Spectator* for May, 1712, and the second appeared independently in the following year.

But a poem which was destined to be more famous than any of these was now in his hands. One of the beaus in London society at this time was Lord Petre, and eminent among the belles was Miss Arabella Fermor. This lady greatly and justly prided herself on two beautiful curls. To possess himself of one of these curls was the cherished object of the said Lord Petre; and, finding that he was not likely to obtain the prize by fair means, he resorted to unfair means, and took the liberty surreptitiously to cut off the curl with a pair of scissors, while the lady was unsuspiciously sipping her coffee. At this she was very naturally indignant, and the result was an estrangement between the family of the Fermors and the family of the Petres. This coming to the ears of a common friend, who was also a friend of Pope—John Caryll—he asked Pope to write some trifle which should turn the whole affair into fun, and laugh the estranged families into amity. With this object Pope composed, in 1711, a little mock heroic poem in two cantos, which was published in *Lintot's Miscellany*, May, 1712, entitled *The Rape of the Lock*. But, happening to fall in with a curious work by the Abbé Villars—*Le Comte de Gabalis*—which gave an account of the mysteries and mythology of the Rosicrucians, he saw how admirably that mythology might be adapted to the purposes of mock heroic poetry. He determined, therefore, against the advice of Addison, to recast and expand his poem. This he did, extending it, chiefly by the introduction of the supernatural machinery, to five cantos; so, in 1714, appeared *The Rape of the Lock* in the form in which we have it now, and English literature was enriched by a masterpiece which has neither equal nor second among mock heroic poems in our own or in any other language. In 1715 appeared the *Temple of Fame*, an adaptation of Chaucer's *House of Fame.*

But Pope was now engaged on a work which left him little leisure for other undertakings. In October, 1713, he had issued proposals for a translation of the *Iliad.* He was anxious to make money, and the composition of original poetry, however much it might add to his fame, was not remunerative. Lintot's account with him has been preserved and shows that for *Windsor Forest* he had only received thirty-two pounds, for the *Essay on Criticism* fifteen, for the first sketch of the *Rape of the Lock* seven, and for the poem in its completed form fifteen. This was not the way to a competency and independence, but a competency and independence Pope determined to secure. He set to work in a manner which did great credit to his abilities for business. The translation was to appear in six volumes, which were to be published at intervals, at a guinea a volume. Shortly after the proposals were issued, he had, thanks to the efforts of Swift and other friends, secured five hundred and seventy-five subscribers, among them the King and the Prince of Wales, some of whom took several copies. This was not all. Bernard Lintot paid twelve hundred pounds for the copyright, supplying gratuitously the copies for the subscribers. The fortunate poet cleared by the *Iliad* upwards of six thousand pounds, a small fortune in those days. It cost him about five years' labour. The first volume was published in June, 1715; the fifth and sixth volumes were published together in May, 1720. The translation of the *Iliad* was so successful that a translation of the *Odyssey* followed naturally. But Pope was weary of drudgery, and it was not till some three years had passed that he betook himself seriously to his new task, and then arranged to divide the labour. Of the *Odyssey* he only translated twelve books; of the other twelve, the first, fourth, nineteenth, and twentieth books were assigned to Elijah Fenton, a poet with a touch of genius; and the second, sixth, eighth, eleventh, twelfth, sixteenth, eighteenth, and twenty-third to William Broome, a respectable scholar and an excellent versifier. The first instalment of the *Odyssey* appeared in the spring of 1725, the last in the summer of 1726. For the *Odyssey* Pope received in all four thousand five hundred pounds, out of which he paid Broome five hundred and Fenton two hundred—not, it must be owned, very liberal remuneration for the assistance they had given him, as he was subsequently more than once reminded. As a translator of Homer, Pope laboured under three great disadvantages: he was very imperfectly acquainted with Greek; he not only lived in an age, but was himself the typical representative of an age, which had scarcely anything in common with the age of the Homeric poems; and, lastly, he had scarcely any of the qualities which constitute the peculiar and essential excellence of the Prince of the Poets of Nature. But, judged as an independent work, it is a memorable and brilliant achievement. Its general character is best indicated by what Bentley and Gibbon said of it: "It is a pretty poem, Mr. Pope, but you must not call it Homer," was Bentley's reply, when Pope asked him whether he had received "his Homer." "It has," says Gibbon, "every merit except that of faithfulness to the original." Coleridge speaks of it as "that astonishing product of talent and ingenuity." As a mercantile speculation it was eminently successful, for by the *Iliad* and the *Odyssey* taken together, Pope cleared at least nine thousand pounds. This sum, judiciously invested and economically managed, not only made him independent for life, but enabled him to surround himself with every social comfort and even luxury at his villa at Twickenham.

> "Thanks to Homer since I live and thrive,
> Indebted to no Prince or Peer alive."
>
> *Imit. of Horace*, Epist. II. ii.

We must now go back a few years to review Pope's life and work while he was engaged in his version of Homer. He had been gradually extending his circle of acquaintance and friends till it embraced many of the leading people of those times, both in the sphere of letters and in the sphere of politics and fashion, as is very gracefully illustrated by Gay's delightful *Welcome from Greece*, a poem dedicated to him on his completion of the version of the *Iliad*. In 1719 he purchased the long lease of a house at Twickenham, with five acres of land, and soon began to amuse himself with adorning and developing his little villa and estate, and with the construction of the famous grotto. In 1717 had appeared his first volume of collected poems, including the *Elegy on an Unfortunate Lady*, and one of the finest and certainly the most pathetic of his poems, *Eloisa to Abelard*, inspired apparently by Lady Mary Wortley Montagu and Miss Martha Blunt, with both of whom he either was, or affected to be, in love. In 1725 appeared his unfortunate edition of Shakespeare, which brought him into collision with Lewis Theobald, the hero of the first editions of the *Dunciad*.

And now commenced the war with the Dunces. Dennis, Ambrose Phillips, and others had long been at enmity with him. The truth seems to have been that Pope was anxious to mark the distinction between himself and the "race that write," the hacks and scribblers whom he and his distinguished friends regarded with disdain. It was certainly a great step from Grub Street and the cocklofts in St. Martin's Lane and the neighbourhood of St. Paul's to the "elegant retreat" at Twickenham, where

> "All the distant din the world can keep
> Rolls o'er my grotto and but soothes my sleep.
> There my retreat the best of patriots grace,
> Chiefs out of war, and statesmen out of place,
> There St. John mingles with my friendly bowl
> The feast of reason and the flow of soul."
>
> *Imit. of Horace*, Sat. II. i.

And yet, as his less fortunate brethren—for brethren

they considered themselves—constantly reminded him, he was no better than themselves—an author by profession. Pope retorted by wishing them dinners, rain-proof garrets, and immunity from bum-bailiffs. Thus it came to pass that he soon numbered among his assailants almost the whole guild of hack authors. The poor wretches fought with such weapons as they had. They circulated the vilest stories about his private life; they taunted him with being a Papist, ridiculed his deformed figure, pulled his Shakespeare and his Homer to pieces, accused him of plagiarism in his poetry, and kept his sensitive spirit constantly on the rack. In 1725-6 Swift visited England, and the first two volumes of the *Miscellanies* were printed, though not published, in June, 1727, the third, containing the *Treatise on the Bathos*, being published in March of that year. This stimulated the malignant activity of the Dunces, and libels and broadsheets directed against Pope and his friends rained down on them like hail. Pope now gave the finishing touches to his great satire, and in May, 1728, the first three books of the *Dunciad* were issued. It was an unequal and ignominious conflict, in which, to employ Gibbon's phrase, victory was a sufficient humiliation. The *Dunciad* is certainly one of the most brilliant of compositions, an astonishing *tour de force*, but it is a lamentable prostitution of genius.

From these wretched controversies Pope was recalled by a friend who had the candour to tell him that he was wasting his superb powers on unworthy objects, and who implored him to consult the interests of his own fame and of posterity. This friend was Bolingbroke, who, having obtained a pardon in 1723, had, in 1724, settled at Dawley, which is within an easy drive of Twickenham. Bolingbroke was then busy with his philosophical writings and speculations, and appears to have been anxious to interest Pope in the same studies. The two men became very intimate, and at Bolingbroke's suggestion Pope embarked on a very ambitious undertaking. This was a great didactic poem, which was to comprise a complete system of ethics, and it was to be in two books: I. Of the Nature and State of Man, with respect to the universe; as an individual; with respect to society; with respect to happiness; II. Of the Use of Things, in nine parts: on the limits of human knowledge, on the use of learning, on the use of wit, on the knowledge and characters of men, on the particular characters of women, on the principle and use of civil and ecclesiastical polity, on the use of education, on the equality of happiness in the several conditions of men, on the use of riches—the whole to have been preceded by an address to the Saviour on the model of the address of Lucretius to Epicurus. Of this ambitious scheme only portions were completed. These portions are represented by the *Essay on Man*, in four epistles, which appeared between 1732 and 1734; the four moral essays which appeared between 1731 and 1735; and the fourth book of the *Dunciad*, published in 1742. That Pope, in attempting a work of this kind, had attempted a work which, if not beyond his strength, was at least not adapted to his powers, is hardly likely to be disputed by any competent judge of the portion which he actually finished. Regarded as a philosophical poem, the *Essay on Man* is almost ridiculous; regarded as a series of fragments, and in relation purely to expression, it is among the most brilliant of Pope's achievements in poetry.

In 1732 John Gay died. Pope was much attached to him, and felt his loss so acutely that for some time he was unable to do any work. When he was thus depressed, Bolingbroke directed his attention to Horace's first Satire of the Second Book, observing how exactly it fitted his case. Pope read the satire, and at once commenced an imitation of it in English. This was the origin of his *Imitations of Horace*, which employed him at intervals between 1732 and 1738. These delightful poems, of which Mark Pattison observes that it is no paradox to say that, "imitations" though they be, they are among the most original of his writings, are seven in number. The Horatian satires and epistles paraphrased are the second Satire of the First Book, published under the title of *Sober Advice from Horace*, and afterwards very properly suppressed, the first and second Satires of the Second Book, the first and sixth Epistles of the First Book, and the two Epistles of the Second Book. In January, 1734-5, appeared the *Epistle to Dr. Arbuthnot*, or, as it was afterwards called, the *Prologue to the Satires*, one of the most brilliant and certainly the most comprehensively characteristic of his poems. Not long before the publication of this work, he became involved in a feud which inspired the severest satire he ever wrote, the character of Sporus inserted in the *Epistle to Dr. Arbuthnot*. His former friendship with Lady Mary Wortley Montagu had turned into virulent hatred, and in the *Imitations of Horace* he had very coarsely libelled her. To revenge herself, she coalesced with her kinsman Lord Hervey, and between them they concocted a satire against Pope, entitled *Verses Addressed to the Imitator of Horace*, in which his character, his family, his figure, and his writings were shamefully assailed. He replied first in prose, in *A Letter to a Noble Lord*, and subsequently inserted, in the *Epistle to Arbuthnot*, the portrait of Hervey, under the title of Sporus, a satire which has no parallel in subtle malignity. In 1738 were published the two Dialogues, which at first took their title from the year, but were afterwards entitled the *Epilogue to the Satires.* In this group of his writings should also be included what he calls *The Satires of Dr. Donne Versified.* These are paraphrases of two of Donne's Satires, namely the second and fourth, but they are not among the most successful of Pope's "imitations."

Meanwhile he had been engaged in those lamentable intrigues, which preceded the publication of his Correspondence in 1737, an episode in his life over which his admirers will always desire to hurry. It may be doubted whether fraud, mendacity, treachery, and meanness ever went further than Pope carried them in this miserable attempt to reconcile dignity with vanity. Briefly, his object was two-fold—to get his Correspondence published, but at the same time to make it appear that the publication had been forced on him in self-defence; and, secondly, to manipulate the Correspondence in such a manner as should add to his literary and social importance.

Pope was now beginning to pay the penalty which advancing years seldom fail to exact from those on whom life has conferred its greatest boons, affection and friendship. In 1733 he lost his beloved mother. In the following year his dear friend Arbuthnot followed. Next went Peterborough, of whom he had written:

> "He whose lightning pierc'd th' Iberian lines,
> Now forms my quincunx, and now ranks my vines,
> Or tames the genius of the stubborn plain,
> Almost as quickly as he conquer'd Spain."
>
> *Imit. of Horace*, Sat. II. i. 129-32.

Swift was lost to him by the increasing infirmities of years and of disease. Of all his old friends, Bolingbroke alone was left. His last years were embittered with an acrimonious feud with Colley Cibber, whom, in an unfortunate moment, he substituted for Theobald as the hero of the *Dunciad*, which was recast for that purpose. In the spring of 1744 it was plain that his health was breaking up. As the year advanced he grew rapidly worse. Some interesting particulars have been given of his last days. Not long before his death he said: "I am so certain of the soul's being immortal that I feel it within me, as it were, by intuition." On being asked by his friend Hooke, a Papist, whether he would not die like his father and mother, and whether a priest should be called, he replied: "I do not think it essential, but it will be very right, and I thank you for putting me in mind of it." He received the last sacraments very devoutly, and observed afterwards: "There is nothing that is meritorious but virtue and friendship, and, indeed, friendship itself is only a part of virtue." He died on the 30th of May, 1744, so peacefully that the attendants did not know the exact moment when he expired. In accordance with the instructions in his will, he was buried in Twickenham Church, near his father and mother.

With all its blemishes there was much which was noble and more which was attractive in Pope's character. In an age of servility, he was sternly and inflexibly independent, in his own words, "unfee'd, unpension'd, no man's heir or slave." Scrupulously true to himself, his soul and his conscience were in his work; and, if labour be prayer, his life was assuredly one long act of devotion.

> "Of his five talents other five he made,
> And heaven that largely gave was largely paid."

In the phrase of a Greek poet, he drove no petty trade with fame, but strove, not for the suffrage of the multitude and of the hour, but for the immortality of a classic. More than once in his poetry and in his correspondence we catch unmistakably the accent of magnanimity—we catch it in the Fourth Epistle of the *Essay on Man*, and in the *Epistle to Oxford in the Tower*, one of the noblest poems of its kind. Nothing can be more touching and beautiful than his affection for his parents and for his friends, nothing more exemplary than his conduct as a son. His liberality and kindness find testimony in numberless grateful tributes from those who knew him in domestic life, and from those who sought his countenance and help in literature. His worst fault was what was indicated by Atterbury, when he described him as *mens curva in corpore curvo*; he was not truthful, he was not candid. Of the malignity and spitefulness which are commonly imputed to him it is only just to say, that they were never exhibited except when provoked.

The best representation of Pope's features is the living bust by Roubilliac; the best description is that given by Sir Joshua Reynolds, who, as a boy, once saw him in an auction room: "He was about four feet six high, very hump-backed, and deformed. He had a very large and very fine eye, and a long handsome nose: his mouth had those peculiar marks which are always found in the mouths of crooked persons; and the muscles which run across the cheeks were so strongly marked as to appear like small cords." The exquisite sensibility thus indicated is the secret of much which has exposed him to censure and misrepresentation.

INTRODUCTION.

It is not possible to determine with certainty the year in which the *Essay on Criticism* was composed. On the title page of the quarto of 1717 it is stated that it was written in 1709, and this statement was repeated in every succeeding edition to the final edition in 1743: it was also corroborated by Pope in one of his conversations with Spence. But he told Richardson that it was written in 1707, and that the printed date, 1709, was a mistake, and he said, practically, the same thing on another occasion to Spence, observing that he had shown the Essay to Walsh the year before Walsh died, and Walsh died in March, 1708. The choice, then, seems to lie between 1707 and 1709, and the balance of probability is in favour of the later date. In any case, it was published anonymously in May, 1711, when Pope was in his twenty-fourth year.

The *Essay on Criticism* belongs to a class of poems which had many precedents both in our own and in other literatures. The earliest example of them is to be found in Horace's *Epistola ad Pisones* or *De Arte Poeticâ Liber*, written probably between 14 and 11 B.C. In this poem Horace deals generally with the principles of composition, in the widest sense of the term, as applied to poetry. After pointing out what is to be aimed at and what is to be avoided in matter, structure, and diction, he goes on to define and characterize the various species of poetry, the style, metre, and treatment proper for each—for tragedy, for comedy, for the epic; discusses how far poetry should be didactic, how far merely amusing; what blemishes are venial, what defects are fatal; the relation of genius to art and of art to genius; dwells on the distinction between the criticism of an interested flatterer and a disinterested and candid judge and adviser; concluding with a picture of a vain and incorrigible poetaster. Fine taste, sound sense, and the nicest critical acumen, the result of long experience and careful study, combine to make this work an invaluable manual both for poets and critics. But this is not the only work in which Horace has discussed critical subjects: to the *Ars Poetica* should be added the Tenth Satire of the First Book and the First Epistle of the Second Book. It would be scarcely possible to overestimate the influence which Horace has exercised, as the author of these poems, on criticism in Europe. He may be regarded not merely as the founder, but as the model and inspirer of the dynasty which has its last eminent representative in Byron.

At the period of the Renaissance Horace found his first successful disciple. In 1527 appeared the *Poetica* of Marco Girolamo Vida, afterwards Bishop of Alba. This is, like the *Ars Poetica*, in Latin hexameters, and was dedicated to the Dauphin, the eldest son of Francis I. The style is modelled not on that of Horace but on that of Virgil, and is not, as in the *Ars Poetica*, easily colloquial, but has the stateliness and pomp of Epic diction. It is more elaborate and methodical than Horace's poem, and is in three books. The first, which draws freely on the *Institutes* of Quintilian and Plutarch's *Treatise on the Training of Children*, describes generally the early education of a poet, and concludes with a declamatory peroration on the dignity and sanctity of poets. The second book describes in detail the characteristics of an ideal epic poem, and is indeed little more than a careful, thoughtful, and tasteful critical analysis of Virgil's *Aeneid*. The subjects treated in the third book are indicated in the opening lines:

> "Nunc autem linguae studium moremque loquendi,
> Quem vates, Musaeque probent, atque auctor Apollo,
> Expediam."

> 'What style, what language, suits the poet's lays,
> To claim Apollo's and the Muses' praise
> I now unfold.'

It is indeed an elaborate treatise on style and diction, borrowing much from Cicero, Horace, Quintilian, and Longinus. The precepts laid down are just and sound, and often very happily expressed and illustrated. That Pope was a careful student of Vida's poems, which later in life he included in his *Selecta Poemata Italorum*, is abundantly evident not only in the *Essay on Criticism* but in the *Rape of the Lock.*

The next important example of this class of poem is Boileau's *L'Art poétique*, published in 1673. This was confessedly modelled on Horace's *Ars Poetica*, and borrowed from Horace its essential and fundamental tenets and canons, the chief of which were the immense importance of form and expression and the substitution of reason and good sense for "enthusiasm" and "rapture."

As Horace had said, "Scribendi recte sapere est et principium et fons," so Boileau repeats (*L'Art*, I. 37-38)·

> "Aimez donc la Raison; que toujours vos écrits
> Empruntent d'elle seule et leur lustre et leur prix."
>
> . . . .
>
> "Tout doit tendre au bon sens."

Boileau's poem is, however, much more elaborate and systematic than Horace's. It is divided into four cantos. The first gives general precepts illustrated with critical remarks on different French poets, from Villon to Malherbe. The second treats of the pastoral, the elegy, the sonnet, the various kinds of lyric poetry, and of satire. The third deals with dramatic poetry and with the epic. The fourth returns again to general precepts, exhorting contemporary poets to respect the dignity of their art, and congratulating them on the propitious times in which it was their lot to live. Few works have had so much influence on criticism as this poem of Boileau. Its popularity was enormous. "He was," says Demogeot, "the teacher of his century; and in his century itself he taught the writers less than the public." Nor is this popularity at all surprising: he gave a voice to the popular taste; his style is admirable—terse, graceful, brilliant, the perfection of precision, finish, and point. He condensed and reproduced all that was best in his master Horace, his fine taste, his sound sense. He has had his reward. "If I may be permitted," says the most distinguished of modern French critics, St. Beuve, "to speak for myself, Boileau is one of the men with whom I have been most occupied since I have been engaged in criticism, and with whom I have most constantly lived in thought." Boileau's work became almost as popular in England as it was in France, for in 1683 a paraphrase adapting its illustrations and allusions to our own literature appeared, the work of Sir William Soame, revised in all probability by Dryden. How carefully Pope had studied it is plain from the numberless reminiscences of it to be found in his Essay. The popularity of Boileau and Horace led to several poems, published between 1679 and the end of the century, dealing with the principles of criticism. In 1679 Sheffield, Earl of Mulgrave, circulated in manuscript his *Essay on Satire*, in which he was probably assisted by Dryden. This was followed in 1682 by his *Essay on Poetry*, in which the influence of Boileau is very evident. The year before (1681) appeared Roscommon's *Essay on Translated Verse*, containing many judicious and sensible remarks, but ludicrously overrated both by Dryden and by Addison. The high opinion entertained of this work by contemporaries is illustrated by Granville's verses:

"First Mulgrave rose, Roscommon next, like light
To clear our darkness and to guide our sight;
With steady judgment and in lofty sounds
They gave us patterns, and they set us bounds;
The Stagirite and Horace laid aside,
Informed by them we seek no other guide."[1]

About this time also Roscommon translated into blank verse Horace's *Ars Poetica*. But these were not the last of these Essays. In or about 1700 George Granville, afterwards Lord Lansdowne, published his *Essay upon Unnatural Flights in Poetry*, written to show that moderation and good sense should be the chief study

[1] *Essay upon Unnatural Flights in Poetry.*

of the true poet. Lastly came the *Essay on Criticism*, in which this species of poetry may be said to culminate. Its significance in relation to what preceded it is indicated by Lady M. Wortley Montagu's remark "that it was all stolen." This is practically the truth. It is the final and concentrated embodiment of what had found expression in all these poets—in Horace, in Vida, in Boileau, in Sheffield, in Roscommon, and in Granville. But it was more than this: it was the result of an intelligent, if somewhat desultory study, of the sources on which some of these poets had themselves drawn, the critical writings, that is to say of Aristotle, Cicero, Dionysius, Quintilian, Longinus, and the works of the English and French critics of the seventeenth century, Bossu, Rapin, Bouhours, and our own Dryden.

From an historical point of view the Essay is of great importance, for it may be said to sum up the canons, tenets, and ideals of that school of poetry known in our literature as the "critical" or "classical" school, the school of which Waller, Denham, Davenant, and Cowley were the forerunners, Dryden the formulator and popularizer, and Pope the most finished representative. And it did more. It reduced chaos to order: it crystallized what was fluid; it defined what was unfixed. It was the first classical contribution to English criticism, the first which attracted universal attention and became authoritative. What the *Book of Sentences* was to the scholastic philosophy of the thirteenth century, this Essay became to the critics of the eighteenth—their manual and their armoury. It is this which accounts for the extravagant eulogies of Addison and Johnson: "The *Essay on Criticism* is," says Johnson, "one of Pope's greatest works, and, if he had written nothing else, it would have placed him among the first critics and first poets, as it exhibits every mode of excellence that can embellish or dignify didactic composition—selection of matter, novelty of arrangement, justness of precept, splendour of illustration, and propriety of digression." Mr. Courthope acutely remarks that "the critical sense of the Essay is most warmly appreciated by those who are nearest to it in point of time, and is coldly spoken of in proportion as the practical value of its maxims becomes less apparent." Thus De Quincey pronounces it to be "the feeblest and least interesting of Pope's writings, being substantially a mere versification, like a metrical multiplication table, of commonplaces the most mouldy with which criticism has baited its rat-traps."[1] This is substantially the judgment also of Mr. Leslie Stephen, though he admits that "it shows singular skill in putting old truths," and hits off "many phrases of marked felicity."

It may be conceded at once that the critical lamps of the eighteenth century are not, and cannot possibly be, the critical lamps of the nineteenth century; and that to go to Pope's Essay for final standards and touchstones would be, in Sancho Panza's phrase, to seek for pears on an elm tree. But it is right that a work should be judged not in relation to what it is not, but in relation to what it is; and there is much, and very much, in the Essay which is of perennial interest and value. Regarding the poem comprehensively, we are confronted with two very opposite conceptions of its scope and purport.

[1] Article on Schlosser's *Literary History of the Eighteenth Century*.

Warburton contends that it is a systematic treatise, and "that no incomplete one, both of the art of Criticism and Poetry"; that it is "a regular piece." Addison, on the other hand, observes that "the observations follow one another, like those in Horace's *Art of Poetry*, without the methodical regularity which would have been requisite in a prose writer"; and De Quincey, going much further than Addison, boldly describes it as "a collection of independent maxims, tied together into a fasciculus by the printer, but having no natural order or logical dependency."[1] The truth obviously lies between these two extremes of opinion. It was not Pope's habit to be logical and coherent. He wrote fragmentarily, finishing couplet by couplet, piece by piece, dove-tailing and connecting each with each, as best he could. His friend Swift very amusingly describes his process of composition:

"Now backs of letters, tho' design'd
 For those who more will need 'em,
Are fill'd with hints and underlin'd,
 Himself can scarcely read 'em.
Each atom to some other struck
 All turns and motions tries;
Till, in a lump together stuck,
 Behold a poem rise."

He produced the *Essay on Criticism* exactly as he produced the *Essay on Man*. Both poems may be compared to mosaic work or patch-work. In the *Essay on Man* he ransacked the writers of all schools, sects, and creeds for his material and philosophy, and consequently produced a poem which is full of contradictions and inconsist-

[1] "Essay on Pope," *Works*, Vol. xv., p. 142.

encies, but which abounds with striking and brilliant passages. His process was the same in composing the *Essay on Criticism*, but, as the principles of criticism are more fixed than the tenets of conflicting philosophic systems, he has not involved himself in the same difficulty. It is probable that, in choosing the term "Essay," —which in Pope's time retained the sense in which it had been employed by Montaigne and Bacon — he intended to indicate the nature of the poem, namely, that it was a contribution, more or less tentative and desultory, to the subject treated in it, not a methodical treatise like Boileau's poem. But method it has, if we do not press details too closely, and more method undoubtedly than Horace's *Art of Poetry.* It is in three parts. The first extends from line 1 to 201, and gives rules for the study of the *Art of Criticism.* It begins by dwelling on the importance of criticism, and the mischief occasioned by its abuse; points out and accounts for the prevalence of bad criticism; and then goes on to show that natural genius, careful discipline, and judiciously directed study must combine to produce a sound and efficient critic; and after commenting on what facilitates and on what impedes in the attainment and use of these requisites, it concludes with an apostrophe to the ancient poets. The second part, from lines 201 to 560, explains the causes of wrong judgment in criticism, which are admirably analyzed and are ten in number: pride, imperfect learning, judging by parts and not by the whole, being too hard to please or too apt to admire, partiality towards the ancients or moderns, prejudice, singularity, inconstancy, party spirit, envy. It then goes on to inculcate the ready recognition of merit; for fame, like life, is brief, and genius has many enemies; but learning at least should be its friend; and the part concludes with some remarks on what a critic may spare or condone, and where he should be unflinchingly severe. The third part, from line 560-744, treats of the Ethics of Criticism: a critic should, in addition to possessing taste, judgment, and learning, be distinguished by candour, modesty, good breeding, and tact. Then are depicted the characters of an incorrigible poet and of an impertinent critic; and next, by way of contrast, the ideal critic. The history of criticism, as illustrated by its most eminent representatives from Aristotle to Walsh, is then briefly reviewed. It will be clear from this that De Quincey's description of the poem is unfair and even absurd; that it has both method and system. If, however, we examine it closely, we shall find that it is full of repetitions, that the statements are not unfrequently inconsistent, and the couplets sometimes inconsequential: a striking instance of this is to be found in lines 33-4, which have absolutely no connection with the context; and in 634-5, which are inconsistent with what is expressed in the preceding couplet. The poem has all the marks of being the work of a young writer. The composition is sometimes stiff, cumbrous, and ungrammatical, as:

> "No monstrous height or breadth or length *appear*," 251

or

> "Neglect the rules each verbal critic *lays*," 261

or

> "In proud dulness joins with quality." 415

or

> "While their weak heads, like towns unfortified,
> 'Twixt sense and nonsense daily change their side."
> 434-5

Nothing could be worse than the following couplet:

> "Nor suffers Horace more in wrong translations,
> By wits, than critics in as wrong quotations." 663-4

The metre is frequently very faulty, and imperfect rhymes abound; thus we find "wit" rhyming with "delight" and with "light," "still" with "suitable," "satires" with "dedicators," "extreme" with "phlegm," "character" with "steer." The rhymes, too, are singularly monotonous: in a poem of 744 lines there are no less than ten couplets rhyming to "sense" and twelve rhyming to "wit."

A more serious objection to the poem lies in its implied underestimate of such poets as Chaucer, Spenser, Shakespeare, and Milton, and its expressed overestimate of such mediocrities as Sheffield, Roscommon, and Walsh. For this seems to indicate that when Pope pronounced Nature to be the supreme pattern and model, and contended that Nature and Homer were the same, he was indulging in mere cant, or was furnished with a criterion which he was unable to apply. His extraordinary estimate of Vida points to the same conclusion. Of one thing there can be no doubt, that with a theory of criticism which must have demonstrated that Dryden and his school were scarcely entitled to the name of poets, he exalted them above all the poets in England. The truth is, that the *Essay on Criticism*, like the *Essay on Man*, was a compilation from different theories of criticism, deriving some of its tenets from a work like the *Ars Poetica*, and some from a work like the *Treatise on the Sublime*. The application of Horace's tests would undoubtedly exalt Dryden above Shakespeare, as the application of those of Longinus would not merely demonstrate the supremacy of Shakespeare, but would almost exclude Dryden from the ranks of poets. Pope's tastes and sympathies were with Horace; when he spoke the language of Longinus he spoke it by rote.

To originality the *Essay on Criticism* has no pretension. It is little more than a *cento*. It may be doubted whether it contains an observation, an idea, an image which is not borrowed. The acquired knowledge displayed in it is, considering the age of the writer, wonderful.

It is, however, no paradox to say that its lack of originality is one of its chief merits. It stands in the same relation to criticism as Bacon's *Essays* stand to ethics and the conduct of life. It is an epitome of tried and useful truths, an anthology of wit and wisdom admirably chosen, admirably presented. It is more than this: it traces feature by feature the portrait of an ideal critic, and the critic who modelled himself on Pope's pattern would, so far as conduct, temper, and general character are concerned, leave little to be desired. St. Beuve has said that every professional critic ought to frame and hang up in his study these lines:

> "But where's the man, who counsel can bestow,
> Still pleas'd to teach, and yet not proud to know?
> Unbiass'd, or by favour, or by spite;
> Not duly prepossess'd, nor blindly right;
> Though learn'd, well-bred; and tho' well-bred, sincere,
> Modestly bold, and humanly severe:
> Who to a friend his faults can freely show,
> And gladly praise the merit of a foe?

Blest with a taste exact, yet unconfin'd;
A knowledge both of books and human kind:
Gen'rous converse; a soul exempt from pride;
And love to praise, with reason on his side?" 630-42

Take again:

"A perfect Judge will read each work of Wit
With the same spirit that its author writ:
Survey the WHOLE, nor seek slight faults to find
Where nature moves and rapture warms the mind;
Nor lose, for that malignant dull delight,
The gen'rous pleasure to be charm'd with Wit."
233-38.

which should be compared with lines 253-67 and lines 384-7. How admirably, too, does he point out in lines 11-14, and in lines 68-74 and 124-35, the relation of natural abilities to discipline, and indicate the most profitable course of study. So, too, in dealing with the ethics of criticism, how excellent are his precepts:

"Good-nature and good-sense must ever join;
To err is human, to forgive, divine." 524-5

"'Tis not enough, taste, judgment, learning, join;
In all you speak, let truth and candour shine:
That not alone what to your sense is due
All may allow; but seek your friendship too." 562-5

"Men must be taught as if you taught them not,
And things unknown propos'd as things forgot.
Without good breeding, truth is disapproved;
That only makes superior sense beloved." 574-7

"'Tis best sometimes your censure to restrain,
And charitably let the dull be vain:
Your silence there is better than your spite,
For who can rail so long as fools can write." 596-9

No one has ever questioned that in terse and felicitous expression Pope has no superior, and very few rivals, among English classics. In his famous definition—true wit

> "Is Nature to advantage dress'd,
> What oft was thought, but ne'er so well express'd;
> Something, whose truth convinc'd at sight we find,
> That gives us back the image of our mind."

—and in this he was a consummate master. Every section of this Essay abounds in aphorisms expressed with final felicity: take a very few out of very many:

> "'Tis with our judgments as our watches, none
> Go just alike, yet each believes his own." 9-10

> "Some have at first for Wits, then Poets past,
> Turn'd Critics next, and prov'd plain fools at last."
> 36-7

> "Great wits sometimes may gloriously offend,
> And rise to faults true Critics dare not mend."
> 159-60

> "Words are like leaves, and where they most abound;
> Much fruit of sense beneath is rarely found." 309-10

> "True ease in writing comes from art, not chance,
> As those move easiest who have learn'd to dance."
> 362-63

> "Envy will merit, as its shade, pursue;
> But like a shadow proves the substance true." 466-7

> "To err is human, to forgive, divine." 525

> "Fools rush in where Angels fear to tread." 625

> "Nor is it Homer nods, but we that dream." 180

Nothing could be more brilliant, eloquent, and felicitous than the simile in which progress in learning is compared to the ascent of the Alps (225-32), or the passage treating of the rhythm and cadence in verse (337-73), or the apostrophe to the Renaissance (697-708).

Weighing the merits with the defects and blemishes of the Essay, an impartial judgment will probably strike the balance between the estimate formed of it by Dr. Johnson and Hazlitt and the estimate formed by De Quincey and Mr. Leslie Stephen. It is not, as the former imply, an original work; it is not a complete treatise, but it is assuredly something more than "a mere versification, like a metrical multiplication table of commonplaces," "hitting off many phrases of marked felicity." Its true position is indicated by St. Beuve. "To my thinking," he says, "it is quite as good as Horace's *Ars Poetica* or Boileau's *Art Poëtique.*" "How many judicious and subtle remarks," he continues, "containing eternal truths do I gather as I read it! With what terseness, conciseness, elegance are they expressed and once for all!" With this verdict, and from such a judge, the admirers of Pope—and they can never become extinct—may well be satisfied.

AN ESSAY ON CRITICISM.

I.

Introduction. That 'tis as great a fault to judge ill as to write ill, and a more dangerous one to the public, v. 1.

That a true Taste *is as rare to be found, as a* true Genius, v. 9 to 18.

That most men are born with some Taste, but spoiled by false Education, v. 19 to 25.

The multitude of Critics, *and causes of them*, v. 26 to 45.

That we are to study our own Taste, *and know the* Limits *of it*, v. 46 to 67.

Nature *the best guide of Judgment*, v. 68 to 87.

Improv'd by Art *and* Rules, *which are but* methodis'd Nature, 88.

Rules *derived from the Practice of the* Ancient Poets, v. id. to 110.

That therefore the Ancients *are necessary to be studyd, by a Critic, particularly* Homer *and* Virgil, v. 120 to 138.

Of Licenses, *and the use of them by the Ancients*, v. 140 to 180.

Reverence due to the Ancients, *and praise of them*, v. 181, *etc.*

'Tis hard to say, if greater want of skill
Appear in writing or in judging ill;
But, of the two, less dang'rous is th' offence
To tire our patience, than mislead our sense.
Some few in that, but numbers err in this,
Ten censure wrong for one who writes amiss;
A fool might once himself alone expose,
Now one in verse makes many more in prose.
'Tis with our judgments as our watches, none
Go just alike, yet each believes his own.
In Poets as true genius is but rare,
True Taste as seldom is the Critic's share;
Both must alike from Heav'n derive their light,
These born to judge, as well as those to write.

Let such teach others who themselves excel,
And censure freely who have written well.
Authors are partial to their wit, 'tis true
But are not critics to their judgment too?
  Yet if we look more closely, we shall find
Most have the seeds of judgment in their mind:
Nature affords at least a glimm'ring light;
The lines, tho' touch'd but faintly, are drawn right.
But as the slightest sketch, if justly trac'd,
Is by ill-colouring but the more disgrac'd,
So by false learning is good sense defac'd:
Some are bewilder'd in the maze of schools,
And some made coxcombs Nature meant but fools.
In search of wit these lose their common sense,
And then turn Critics in their own defence:
Each burns alike, who can, or cannot write,
Or with a Rival's, or an Eunuch's spite.
All fools have still an itching to deride,
And fain would be upon the laughing side.
If Mævius scribble in Apollo's spite,
There are who judge still worse than he can write.
  Some have at first for Wits, then Poets past,
Turn'd Critics next, and prov'd plain fools at last.
Some neither can for Wits nor Critics pass,
As heavy mules are neither horse nor ass.
Those half-learn'd witlings, num'rous in our isle,
As half-form'd insects on the banks of Nile;
Unfinish'd things, one knows not what to call,
Their generation's so equivocal:
To tell 'em, would a hundred tongues require,
Or one vain wit's, that might a hundred tire.
  But you who seek to give and merit fame,
And justly bear a Critic's noble name,
Be sure yourself and your own reach to know,
How far your genius, taste, and learning go;
Launch not beyond your depth, but be discreet,

And mark that point where sense and dulness meet.
 Nature to all things fix'd the limits fit,
And wisely curb'd proud man's pretending wit.
As on the land while here the ocean gains,
In other parts it leaves wide sandy plains;
Thus in the soul while memory prevails,
The solid pow'r of understanding fails;
Where beams of warm imagination play,
The memory's soft figures melt away.
One science only will one genius fit;
So vast is art, so narrow human wit:
Not only bounded to peculiar arts,
But oft in those confin'd to single parts.
Like kings we lose the conquests gain'd before,
By vain ambition still to make them more;
Each might his sev'ral province well command,
Would all but stoop to what they understand.
 First follow Nature, and your judgment frame
By her just standard, which is still the same:
Unerring NATURE, still divinely bright,
One clear, unchang'd, and universal light,
Life, force, and beauty, must to all impart,
At once the source, and end, and test of Art.
Art from that fund each just supply provides,
Works without show, and without pomp presides:
In some fair body thus th' informing soul
With spirits feeds, with vigour fills the whole,
Each motion guides, and ev'ry nerve sustains;
Itself unseen, but in th' effects, remains.
Some, to whom Heav'n in wit has been profuse,
Want as much more, to turn it to its use;
For wit and judgment often are at strife,
Tho' meant each other's aid, like man and wife.
'Tis more to guide, than spur the Muse's steed;
Restrain his fury, than provoke his speed;
The winged courser, like a gen'rous horse,

Shows most true mettle when you check his course.
Those RULES of old discovered, not devis'd,
Are Nature still, but Nature methodiz'd;
Nature, like liberty, is but restrain'd
By the same laws which first herself ordain'd.
Hear how learn'd Greece her useful rules indites,
When to repress, and when indulge our flights:
High on Parnassus' top her sons she show'd,
And pointed out those arduous paths they trod;
Held from afar, aloft, th' immortal prize,
And urg'd the rest by equal steps to rise.
Just precepts thus from great examples giv'n,
She drew from them what they deriv'd from Heav'n.
The gen'rous Critic fann'd the Poet's fire,
And taught the world with reason to admire.
Then Criticism the Muse's handmaid prov'd,
To dress her charms, and make her more belov'd:
But following wits from that intention stray'd,
Who could not win the mistress, woo'd the maid;
Against the Poets their own arms they turn'd,
Sure to hate most the men from whom they learn'd.
So modern 'Pothecaries, taught the art
By Doctor's bills to play the Doctor's part,
Bold in the practice of mistaken rules,
Prescribe, apply, and call their masters fools.
Some on the leaves of ancient authors prey,
Nor time nor moths e'er spoil'd so much as they.
Some drily plain, without invention's aid,
Write dull receipts how poems may be made.
These leave the sense, their learning to display,
And those explain the meaning quite away.
You then whose judgment the right course would steer,
Know well each ANCIENT's proper character;
His fable, subject, scope in ev'ry page;
Religion, Country, genius of his Age:
Without all these at once before your eyes,

Cavil you may, but never criticize.
Be Homer's works your study and delight,
Read them by day, and meditate by night;
Thence form your judgment, thence your maxims bring,
And trace the Muses upward to their spring.
Still with itself compar'd, his text peruse;
And let your comment be the Mantuan Muse.
When first young Maro in his boundless mind
A work t' outlast immortal Rome design'd,
Perhaps he seem'd above the critic's law,
And but from Nature's fountains scorn'd to draw:
But when t' examine ev'ry part he came,
Nature and Homer were, he found, the same.
Convinc'd, amaz'd, he checks the bold design;
And rules as strict his labour'd work confine,
As if the Stagirite o'erlook'd each line.
Learn hence for ancient rules a just esteem;
To copy Nature is to copy them.
Some beauties yet no Precepts can declare,
For there's a happiness as well as care.
Music resembles Poetry, in each
Are nameless graces which no methods teach,
And which a master-hand alone can reach.
If, where the rules not far enough extend,
(Since rules were made but to promote their end)
Some lucky Licence answer to the full
Th' intent propos'd, that Licence is a rule.
Thus Pegasus, a nearer way to take,
May boldly deviate from the common track;
From vulgar bounds with brave disorder part,
And snatch a grace beyond the reach of art,
Which without passing thro' the judgment, gains
The heart, and all its end at once attains.
In prospects thus, some objects please our eyes,
Which out of nature's common order rise,
The shapeless rock, or hanging precipice.

Great wits sometimes may gloriously offend,
And rise to faults true Critics dare not mend,
But tho' the Ancients thus their rules invade.
(As Kings dispense with laws themselves have made)
Moderns, beware! or if you must offend
Against the precept, ne'er transgress its End;
Let it be seldom, and compell'd by need;
And have, at least, their precedent to plead.
The Critic else proceeds without remorse,
Seizes your fame, and puts his laws in force.
I know there are, to whose presumptuous thoughts
Those freer beauties, ev'n in them, seem faults.
Some figures monstrous and mis-shap'd appear,
Consider'd singly, or beheld too near,
Which, but proportion'd to their light, or place,
Due distance reconciles to form and grace.
A prudent chief not always must display
His pow'rs in equal ranks, and fair array.
But with th' occasion and the place comply,
Conceal his force, nay seem sometimes to fly.
Those oft are stratagems which error seem,
Nor is it Homer nods, but we that dream.
Still green with bays each ancient Altar stands,
Above the reach of sacrilegious hands;
Secure from Flames, from Envy's fiercer rage,
Destructive War, and all-involving Age.
See, from each clime the learn'd their incense bring!
Hear, in all tongues consenting Pæans ring!
In praise so just let ev'ry voice be join'd,
And fill the gen'ral chorus of mankind.
Hail, Bards triumphant! born in happier days;
Immortal heirs of universal praise!
Whose honours with increase of ages grow,
As streams roll down, enlarging as they flow;
Nations unborn your mighty names shall sound,
And worlds applaud that must not yet be found!

Oh may some spark of your celestial fire,
The last, the meanest of your sons inspire,
(That on weak wings, from far, pursues your flights;
Glows while he reads, but trembles as he writes)
To teach vain Wits a science little known,
T' admire superior sense, and doubt their own!

II.

Causes hindering a true Judgment. 1. Pride, v. 208. 2. Imperfect Learning, v. 215. 3. *Judging by* parts, *and not by the whole*, v. 233 to 288. *Critics in* Wit, Language, Versification, *only*, v. 288, 305, 339, etc. 4. *Being too hard to please, or too apt to admire*, v. 384. 5. Partiality—*too much Love to a Sect,—to the* Ancients *or* Moderns, v. 394. 6. Prejudice *or* Prevention, v. 408. 7. Singularity, v. 424. 8. Inconstancy, v. 430. 9. Party Spirit, v. 452, etc. 10. Envy, v. 466. *Against Envy, and in praise of Good-nature*, v. 508, etc. *When Severity is chiefly to be used by Critics*, v. 526, etc.

Of all the Causes which conspire to blind
Man's erring judgment, and misguide the mind,
What the weak head with strongest bias rules,
Is *Pride*, the never-failing voice of fools.
Whatever nature has in worth denied,
She gives in large recruits of needful pride;
For as in bodies, thus in souls, we find
What wants in blood and spirits, swell'd with wind:
Pride, where wit fails, steps in to our defence,
And fills up all the mighty Void of sense.
If once right reason drives that cloud away,
Truth breaks upon us with resistless day.
Trust not yourself; but your defects to know,
Make use of ev'ry friend—and ev'ry foe.
A little learning is a dang'rous thing;
Drink deep, or taste not the Pierian spring:
There shallow draughts intoxicate the brain,
And drinking largely sobers us again.
Fir'd at first sight with what the Muse imparts,

In fearless youth we tempt the heights of Arts,
While from the bounded level of our mind
Short views we take, nor see the lengths behind ;
But more advanc'd, behold with strange surprise
New distant scenes of endless science rise !
So pleas'd at first the tow'ring Alps we try
Mount o'er the vales, and seem to tread the sky,
Th' eternal snows appear already past,
And the first clouds and mountains seem the last ;
But, those attain'd, we tremble to survey
The growing labours of the lengthen'd way,
Th' increasing prospect tires our wand'ring eyes,
Hills peep o'er hills, and Alps on Alps arise !
  A perfect Judge will read each work of Wit
With the same spirit that its author writ :
Survey the WHOLE, nor seek slight faults to find
Where nature moves, and rapture warms the mind ;
Nor lose, for that malignant dull delight,
The gen'rous pleasure to be charm'd with Wit.
But in such lays as neither ebb, nor flow,
Correctly cold, and regularly low,
That shunning faults one quiet tenour keep ;
We cannot blame indeed—but we may sleep.
In wit, as nature, what affects our hearts
Is not th' exactness of peculiar parts ;
'Tis not a lip, or eye, we beauty call,
But the joint force and full result of all.
Thus when we view some well-proportion'd dome,
(The world's just wonder, and ev'n thine, O Rome !)
No single parts unequally surprise,
All comes united to th' admiring eyes ;
No monstrous height, or breadth, or length appear ;
The Whole at once is bold, and regular.
  Whoever thinks a faultless piece to see,
Thinks what ne'er was, nor is, nor e'er shall be.
In every work regard the writer's End,

Since none can compass more than they intend ;
And if the means be just, the conduct true,
Applause, in spite of trivial faults, is due ;
As men of breeding, sometimes men of wit,
T' avoid great errors, must the less commit :
Neglect the rules each verbal Critic lays,
For not to know some trifles, is a praise.
Most Critics, fond of some subservient art,
Still make the Whole depend upon a Part :
They talk of principles, but notions prize,
And all to one lov'd Folly sacrifice.
  Once on a time, La Mancha's Knight, they say,
A certain bard encount'ring on the way,
Discours'd in terms as just, with looks as sage,
As e'er could Dennis of the Grecian stage ;
Concluding all were desp'rate sots and fools,
Who durst depart from Aristotle's rules.
Our Author, happy in a judge so nice,
Produc'd his Play, and begg'd the Knight's advice :
Made him observe the subject, and the plot,
The manners, passions, unities ; what not ?
All which, exact to rule, were brought about,
Were but a Combat in the lists left out.
"What ! leave the Combat out ?" exclaims the Knight ;
Yes, or we must renounce the Stagirite.
"Not so by Heav'n" (he answers in a rage),
"Knights, squires, and steeds, must enter on the stage."
So vast a throng the stage can ne'er contain.
"Then build a new, or act it in a plain."
  Thus Critics, of less judgment than caprice,
Curious not knowing, not exact but nice,
Form short Ideas ; and offend in arts
(As most in manners) by a love to parts.
  Some to *Conceit* alone their taste confine,
And glitt'ring thoughts struck out at ev'ry line ;
Pleas'd with a work where nothing's just or fit ;

One glaring Chaos and wild heap of wit.
Poets like painters, thus, unskill'd to trace
The naked nature and the living grace,
With gold and jewels cover ev'ry part,
And hide with ornaments their want of art.
True Wit is Nature to advantage dress'd,
What oft was thought, but ne'er so well express'd;
Something, whose truth convinc'd at sight we find,
That gives us back the image of our mind.
As shades more sweetly recommend the light,
So modest plainness sets off sprightly wit.
For works may have more wit than does 'em good,
As bodies perish thro' excess of blood.
  Others for *Language* all their care express,
And value books, as women men, for Dress:
Their praise is still,—the Style is excellent:
The Sense, they humbly take upon content.
Words are like leaves; and where they most abound,
Much fruit of sense beneath is rarely found,
False Eloquence, like the prismatic glass,
Its gaudy colours spreads on ev'ry place;
The face of Nature we no more survey,
All glares alike, without distinction gay:
But true expression, like th' unchanging Sun,
Clears and improves whate'er it shines upon,
It gilds all objects but it alters none.
Expression is the dress of thought, and still
Appears more decent, as more suitable;
A vile conceit in pompous words express'd,
Is like a clown in regal purple dress'd:
For diff'rent styles with diff'rent subjects sort,
As several garbs with country, town, and court.
Some by old words to fame have made pretence,
Ancients in phrase, mere moderns in their sense;
Such labour'd nothings, in so strange a style,
Amaze th' unlearn'd, and make the learned smile.

Unlucky, as Fungoso in the play,
These sparks with awkward vanity display
What the fine gentleman wore yesterday ;
And but so mimic ancient wits at best,
As apes our grandsires, in their doublets drest.
In words, as fashions, the same rule will hold ;
Alike fantastic, if too new, or old :
Be not the first by whom the new are try'd,
Nor yet the last to lay the old aside.
But most by Numbers judge a Poet's song ;
And smooth or rough, with them is right or wrong :
In the bright Muse though thousand charms conspire,
Her voice is all these tuneful fools admire ;
Who haunt Parnassus but to please their ear,
Not mend their minds ; as some to Church repair,
Not for the doctrine, but the music there.
These equal syllables alone require,
Tho' oft the ear the open vowels tire ;
While expletives their feeble aid do join ;
And ten low words oft creep in one dull line :
While they ring round the same unvary'd chimes,
With sure returns of still expected rhymes ;
Where-e'er you find "the cooling western breeze,"
In the next line, it "whispers through the trees" :
If crystal streams "with pleasing murmurs creep,"
The reader's threaten'd (not in vain) with "sleep" :
Then, at the last and only couplet fraught
With some unmeaning thing they call a thought,
A needless Alexandrine ends the song
That, like a wounded snake, drags its slow length along.
Leave such to tune their own dull rhymes, and know
What's roundly smooth or languishingly slow ;
And praise the easy vigour of a line,
Where Denham's strength, and Waller's sweetness join.
True ease in writing comes from art, not chance,
As those move easiest who have learn'd to dance.

'Tis not enough no harshness gives offence,
The sound must seem an Echo to the sense:
Soft is the strain when Zephyr gently blows,
And the smooth stream in smoother numbers flows;
But when loud surges lash the sounding shore,
The hoarse, rough verse should like the torrent roar:
When Ajax strives some rock's vast weight to throw,
The line too labours, and the words move slow;
Not so, when swift Camilla scours the plain,
Flies o'er th' unbending corn, and skims along the main.
Hear how Timotheus' varied lays surprise,
And bid alternate passions fall and rise!
While, at each change, the son of Libyan Jove
Now burns with glory, and then melts with love,
Now his fierce eyes with sparkling fury glow,
Now sighs steal out, and tears begin to flow:
Persians and Greeks like turns of nature found,
And the world's victor stood subdu'd by Sound!
The pow'r of Music all our hearts allow,
And what Timotheus was, is DRYDEN now.
Avoid Extremes; and shun the fault of such,
Who still are pleas'd too little or too much.
At ev'ry trifle scorn to take offence,
That always shows great pride, or little sense;
Those heads, as stomachs, are not sure the best,
Which nauseate all, and nothing can digest.
Yet let not each gay Turn thy rapture move;
For fools admire, but men of sense approve:
As things seem large which we thro' mists descry,
Dulness is ever apt to magnify.
Some foreign writers, some our own despise;
The Ancients only, or the Moderns prize.
Thus Wit, like Faith, by each man is apply'd
To one small sect, and all are damn'd beside.
Meanly they seek the blessing to confine,
And force that sun but on a part to shine,

Which not alone the southern wit sublimes,
But ripens spirits in cold northern climes;
Which from the first has shone on ages past,
Enlights the present, and shall warm the last;
Tho' each may feel increases and decays,
And see now clearer and now darker days.
Regard not then if Wit be old or new,
But blame the false, and value still the true.
  Some ne'er advance a Judgment of their own,
But catch the spreading notion of the Town;
They reason and conclude by precedent,
And own stale nonsense which they ne'er invent.
Some judge of authors' names, not works, and then
Nor praise nor blame the writings, but the men.
Of all this servile herd the worst is he
That in proud dulness joins with Quality.
A constant Critic at the great man's board.
To fetch and carry nonsense for my Lord.
What woful stuff this madrigal would be,
In some starv'd hackney sonneteer, or me?
But let a Lord once own the happy lines,
How the wit brightens! how the style refines!
Before his sacred name flies ev'ry fault,
And each exalted stanza teems with thought!
  The Vulgar thus through Imitation err;
As oft the Learn'd by being singular;
So much they scorn the crowd, that if the throng
By chance go right, they purposely go wrong;
So Schismatics the plain believers quit,
And are but damn'd for having too much wit.
Some praise at morning what they blame at night;
But always think the last opinion right.
A Muse by these is like a mistress us'd,
This hour she's idoliz'd, the next abus'd;
While their weak heads like towns unfortify'd,
'Twixt sense and nonsense daily change their side.

Ask them the cause; they're wiser still, they say;
And still to-morrow's wiser than to-day.
We think our fathers fools, so wise we grow,
Our wiser sons, no doubt, will think us so.
Once School-divines this zealous isle o'erspread;
Who knew most Sentences, was deepest read;
Faith, Gospel, all, seem'd made to be disputed.
And none had sense enough to be confuted:
Scotists and Thomists, now, in peace remain,
Amidst their kindred cobwebs in Duck-lane.
If faith itself has diff'rent dresses worn,
What wonder modes in Wit should take their turn?
Oft', leaving what is natural and fit,
The current folly proves the ready wit;
And authors think their reputation safe,
Which lives as long as fools are pleas'd to laugh.
  Some valuing those of their own side or mind,
Still make themselves the measure of mankind:
Fondly we think we honour merit then,
When we but praise ourselves in other men.
Parties in Wit attend on those of State,
And public faction doubles private hate.
Pride, Malice, Folly, against Dryden rose,
In various shapes of Parsons, Critics, Beaus;
But sense surviv'd, when merry jests were past;
For rising merit will buoy up at last.
Might he return, and bless once more our eyes,
New Blackmores and new Milbourns must arise:
Nay should great Homer lift his awful head,
Zoilus again would start up from the dead.
Envy will merit, as its shade, pursue;
But like a shadow, proves the substance true;
For envy'd Wit, like Sol eclips'd, makes known
Th' opposing body's grossness, not its own,
When first that sun too pow'rful beams displays,
It draws up vapours which obscure its rays;

But ev'n those clouds at last adorn its way,
Reflect new glories and augment the day.
Be thou the first true merit to befriend;
His praise is lost, who stays, till all commend.
Short is the date, alas, of modern rhymes,
And 'tis but just to let them live betimes.
No longer now that golden age appears,
When Patriarch-wits surviv'd a thousand years:
Now length of Fame (our second life) is lost,
And bare threescore is all ev'n that can boast;
Our sons their fathers' failing language see,
And such as Chaucer is, shall Dryden be.
So when the faithful pencil has design'd
Some bright Idea of the master's mind,
Where a new world leaps out at his command,
And ready Nature waits upon his hand;
When the ripe colours soften and unite,
And sweetly melt into just shade and light;
When mellowing years their full perfection give,
And each bold figure just begins to live,
The treach'rous colours the fair art betray,
And all the bright creation fades away!
Unhappy Wit, like most mistaken things,
Atones not for that envy which it brings.
In youth alone its empty praise we boast,
But soon the short-liv'd vanity is lost:
Like some fair flow'r the early spring supplies,
That gaily blooms, but ev'n in blooming dies.
What is this Wit, which must our cares employ?
The owner's wife, that other men enjoy;
Then most our trouble still when most admir'd,
And still the more we give, the more requir'd;
Whose fame with pains we guard, but lose with ease,
Sure some to vex, but never all to please;
'Tis what the vicious fear, the virtuous shun,
By fools 'tis hated, and by knaves undone!

If Wit so much from Ign'rance undergo,
Ah let not Learning too commence its foe!
Of old, those met rewards who could excel,
And such were prais'd who but endeavour'd well:
Tho' triumphs were to gen'rals only due,
Crowns were reserv'd to grace the soldiers too.
Now, they who reach Parnassus' lofty crown,
Employ their pains to spurn some others down;
And while self-love each jealous writer rules,
Contending wits become the sport of fools:
But still the worst with most regret commend,
For each ill Author is as bad a Friend.
To what base ends, and by what abject ways,
Are mortals urg'd thro' sacred lust of praise!
Ah ne'er so dire a thirst of glory boast,
Nor in the Critic let the Man be lost.
Good-nature and good-sense must ever join;
To err is human, to forgive, divine.
But if in noble minds some dregs remain
Not yet purg'd off, of spleen and sour disdain;
Discharge that rage on more provoking crimes,
Nor fear a dearth in these flagitious times.
No pardon vile Obscenity should find,
Tho' wit and art conspire to move your mind;
But Dulness with Obscenity must prove
As shameful, sure, as Impotence in love.
In the fat age of pleasure, wealth, and ease,
Sprung the rank weed, and thriv'd with large increase:
When love was all an easy Monarch's care;
Seldom at council, never in a war:
Jilts rul'd the state, and statesmen farces writ;
Nay wits had pensions, and young Lords had wit:
The Fair sate panting at a Courtier's play,
And not a Mask went unimprov'd away:
The modest fan was lifted up no more,
And Virgins smil'd at what they blush'd before.

The following licence of a Foreign reign
Did all the dregs of bold Socinus drain;
Then unbelieving priests reform'd the nation,
And taught more pleasant methods of salvation;
Where Heav'n's free subjects might their rights dispute,
Lest God himself should seem too absolute:
Pulpits their sacred satire learn'd to spare,
And Vice admir'd to find a flatt'rer there!
Encourag'd thus, Wit's Titans brav'd the skies,
And the press groan'd with licens'd blasphemies.
These monsters, Critics! with your darts engage,
Here point your thunder, and exhaust your rage!
Yet shun their fault, who, scandalously nice,
Will needs mistake an author into vice;
All seems infected that th' infected spy,
As all looks yellow to the jaundic'd eye.

III.

Rules for the Conduct of Manners *in a Critic.* 1. Candour, v. 563. Modesty, v. 566. Good-breeding, v. 572. Sincerity, *and* Freedom *of advice*, v. 578. 2. *When one's Counsel is to be restrained*, v. 584. *Character of an* incorrigible Poet, v. 600. *And of an* impertinent Critic, v. 610, etc. *Character of a* good Critic, v. 629. *The* History *of* Criticism, *and Characters of the best Critics*, Aristotle, v. 645. Horace, v. 653. Dionysius, v. 665. Petronius, v. 667. Quintilian, v. 670. Longinus, v. 675. *Of the Decay of Criticism, and its Revival.* Erasmus, v. 693. Vida, v. 705. Boileau, v. 714. *Lord* Roscommon, *etc.* v. 725. *Conclusion.*

Learn then what Morals Critics ought to show,
For 'tis but half a Judge's task, to know.
'Tis not enough, taste, judgment, learning, join;
In all you speak, let truth and candour shine:
That not alone what to your sense is due
All may allow; but seek your friendship too.
Be silent always when you doubt your sense;
And speak, tho' sure, with seeming diffidence:

Some positive, persisting fops we know,
Who, if once wrong, will needs be always so;
But you, with pleasure own your errors past,
And make each day a Critic on the last.
'Tis not enough, your counsel still be true;
Blunt truths more mischief than nice falsehoods do;
Men must be taught as if you taught them not,
And things unknown propos'd as things forgot.
Without Good Breeding, truth is disapprov'd:
That only makes superior sense belov'd.
Be niggards of advice on no pretence;
For the worst avarice is that of sense.
With mean complacence ne'er betray your trust,
Nor be so civil as to prove unjust.
Fear not the anger of the wise to raise:
Those best can bear reproof, who merit praise.
'Twere well might critics still this freedom take,
But Appius reddens at each word you speak,
And stares, tremendous, with a threat'ning eye,
Like some fierce Tyrant in old tapestry.
Fear most to tax an Honourable fool,
Whose right it is, uncensur'd, to be dull;
Such, without wit, are Poets when they please,
As without learning they can take Degrees.
Leave dang'rous truths to unsuccessful Satires,
And flattery to fulsome Dedicators,
Whom, when they praise, the world believes no more,
Than when they promise to give scribbling o'er.
'Tis best sometimes your censure to restrain,
And charitably let the dull be vain:
Your silence there is better than your spite,
For who can rail so long as they can write?
Still humming on, their drowsy course they keep,
And lash'd so long, like tops, are lash'd asleep.
False steps but help them to renew the race,
As, after stumbling, Jades will mend their pace.

What crowds of these, impenitently bold,
In sounds and jingling syllables grown old,
Still run on Poets, in a raging vein,
Ev'n to the dregs and squeezings of the brain,
Strain out the last dull droppings of their sense,
And rhyme with all the rage of Impotence.
Such shameless Bards we have ; and yet 'tis true,
There are as mad, abandon'd Critics too.
The bookful blockhead, ignorantly read,
With loads of learned lumber in his head,
With his own tongue still edifies his ears,
And always list'ning to himself appears.
All books he reads, and all he reads assails,
From Dryden's Fables down to Durfey's Tales.
With him, most authors steal their works, or buy ;
Garth did not write his own Dispensary.
Name a new Play, and he's the Poet's friend,
Nay show'd his faults—but when would Poets mend?
No place so sacred from such fops is barr'd,
Nor is Paul's church more safe than Paul's churchyard :
Nay, fly to Altars ; there they'll talk you dead ;
For Fools rush in where Angels fear to tread.
Distrustful sense with modest caution speaks,
It still looks home, and short excursions makes ;
But rattling nonsense in full volleys breaks,
And never shock'd, and never turn'd aside,
Bursts out, resistless, with a thund'ring tide.
But where's the man, who counsel can bestow,
Still pleas'd to teach, and yet not proud to know?
Unbiass'd, or by favour, or by spite ;
Not dully prepossess'd, nor blindly right
Tho' learn'd, well-bred ; and tho' well-bred, sincere,
Modestly bold, and humanly severe :
Who to a friend his faults can freely show,
And gladly praise the merit of a foe?
Blest with a taste exact, yet unconfin'd ;

A knowledge both of books and human kind:
Gen'rous converse; a soul exempt from pride;
And love to praise, with reason on his side?
  Such once were Critics; such the happy few,
Athens and Rome in better ages knew.
The mighty Stagirite first left the shore,
Spread all his sails, and durst the deeps explore:
He steer'd securely, and discover'd far,
Led by the light of the Maeonian Star.
Poets, a race long unconfin'd, and free,
Still fond and proud of savage liberty,
Received his laws; and stood convinc'd 'twas fit,
Who conquer'd Nature, should preside o'er Wit.
  Horace still charms with graceful negligence,
And without method talks us into sense,
Will, like a friend, familiarly convey
The truest notions in the easiest way.
He, who supreme in judgment, as in wit,
Might boldly censure, as he boldly writ,
Yet judg'd with coolness, tho' he sung with fire;
His Precepts teach but what his works inspire.
Our Critics take a contrary extreme,
They judge with fury, but they write with phlegm:
Nor suffers Horace more in wrong Translations
By Wits, than Critics in as wrong Quotations.
  See Dionysius Homer's thoughts refine,
And call new beauties forth from ev'ry line!
  Fancy and art in gay Petronius please,
The scholar's learning, with the courtier's ease.
  In grave Quintilian's copious work, we find
The justest rules, and clearest method join'd:
Thus useful arms in magazines we place,
All rang'd in order, and dispos'd with grace,
But less to please the eye, than arm the hand,
Still fit for use, and ready at command.
  Thee, bold Longinus! all the Nine inspire,

And bless their Critic with a Poet's fire.
An ardent Judge, who zealous in his trust,
With warmth gives sentence, yet is always just;
Whose own example strengthens all his laws;
And is himself that great Sublime he draws.
  Thus long succeeding Critics justly reign'd,
Licence repress'd, and useful laws ordain'd.
Learning and Rome alike in empire grew;
And Arts still follow'd where her Eagles flew;
From the same foes, at last, both felt their doom,
And the same age saw Learning fall, and Rome.
With Tyranny, then Superstition join'd,
As that the body, this enslav'd the mind;
Much was believ'd, but little understood,
And to be dull was constru'd to be good;
A second deluge Learning thus o'er-run,
And the Monks finish'd what the Goths begun.
  At length Erasmus, that great injur'd name,
(The glory of the Priesthood, and the Shame!)
Stemm'd the wild torrent of a barb'rous age,
And drove those holy Vandals off the stage.
  But see! each Muse, in LEO's golden days,
Starts from her trance, and trims her wither'd bays,
Rome's ancient Genius, o'er its ruins spread,
Shakes off the dust, and rears his rev'rend head.
Then Sculpture and her sister-arts revive;
Stones leap'd to form, and rocks began to live;
With sweeter notes each rising Temple rung;
A Raphael painted, and a Vida sung.
Immortal Vida: on whose honour'd brow
The Poet's bays and Critic's ivy grow:
Cremona now shall ever boast thy name,
As next in place to Mantua, next in fame!
  But soon by impious arms from Latium chas'd,
Their ancient bounds the banish'd Muses pass'd;
Thence Arts o'er all the northern world advance,

But Critic-learning flourish'd most in France :
The rules a nation, born to serve, obeys ;
And Boileau still in right of Horace sways.
But we, brave Britons, foreign laws despis'd,
And kept unconquer'd, and unciviliz'd ;
Fierce for the liberties of wit, and bold,
We still defy'd the Romans, as of old.
Yet some there were, among the sounder few
Of those who less presum'd, and better knew,
Who durst assert the juster ancient cause,
And here restor'd Wit's fundamental laws.
Such was the Muse, whose rules and practice tell,
"Nature's chief Master-piece is writing well."
Such was Roscommon, not more learn'd than good,
With manners gen'rous as his noble blood ;
To him the wit of Greece and Rome was known,
And ev'ry author's merit, but his own.
Such late was Walsh—the Muse's judge and friend,
Who justly knew to blame or to commend ;
To failings mild, but zealous for desert ;
The clearest head, and the sincerest heart.
This humble praise, lamented shade ! receive,
This praise at least a grateful Muse may give :
The Muse, whose early voice you taught to sing,
Prescrib'd her heights, and prun'd her tender wing,
(Her guide now lost) no more attempts to rise,
But in low numbers short excursions tries :
Content, if hence th' unlearn'd their wants may view,
The learn'd reflect on what before they knew :
Careless of censure, nor too fond of fame ;
Still pleas'd to praise, yet not afraid to blame,
Averse alike to flatter, or offend ;
Not free from faults, nor yet too vain to mend.

NOTES.

I.

4. **sense**, that is perception, faculty of critical appreciation.

5. **in that ... in this**, in tiring our patience by bad writing, in misleading our sense by 'judging ill.'

6. **censure.** The word censure (directly from the Lat. *censeo*), properly means to weigh or estimate, to form a judgment of a thing, and as judgments are often unfavourable, it came to mean to blame or reprimand, and that meaning it often had in Pope's time, and always has now.

9. **'Tis with our judgments as our watches.** This very ingenious simile was perhaps suggested by a passage in Sir John Suckling's epilogue to his tragi-comedy *Aglaura*:

> "But as when an authentic watch is shown,
> Each man winds up and rectifies his own,
> So in our very judgments."

But Pope has given it quite another turn.

11. **In Poets as true genius**, etc. Pope, following Longinus, places a great critic almost on the same level as a great original genius. Both must be born and not simply made, both "derive their light from heaven." This is probably not far from the truth; for taste, the essential characteristic of the true critic, and genius, the essential characteristic of the true artist, are essentially but one faculty: genius is taste in its creative impulse, taste is genius in its elective energy. Johnson, in his Life of Cowley, defines a true genius as "a mind of large general powers accidentally determined in some particular direction," but modern subtlety distinguishes between genius and talent: for which see De Quincey (Article on Keat's Works, Vol. v., p. 275, and Autobiographical Sketches, *Works*, Vol. XIV., 198), and Lord Lytton's famous lines beginning:

> "Talent convinces, genius but excites;
> This takes the reason, that the soul delights," etc.

15, 16. **Let such teach others.** In the English of the sixteenth, seventeenth, and eighteenth centuries, 'who' is commonly used as the correlative of 'such,' as in this poem in lines 385 and 511. There is an ambiguity in the expression 'themselves excel,' themselves is of course the nominative not the objective case. As an illustration of his remark Pope quotes from Pliny: "De pictore, sculptore, fictore nisi artifex judicare non potest," only an artist can pass judgment on a painter, sculptor, and statuary. Mr. Elwin quotes Addison, *Tatler*, Oct. 19th, 1710: "It is ridiculous for any man to criticise the works of another who has not distinguished himself by his own performances." But Johnson's robust good sense was nearer the mark when he said, with reference to a similar remark: "This is not just reasoning. You may abuse a tragedy though you cannot write one. You may scold a carpenter who has made you a bad table though y. cannot make a table. It is not your trade to make tables."—Croker's *Boswell's Johnson*, p. 139. Still, we cannot but feel with Serjeant Maynard, who was fond of saying, "Felices essent artes, si nulli de eis judicarent nisi artifices," 'Happy would the arts be if none but connoisseurs were their critics.'

17. **wit.** This word occurs some forty-six times in the course of the poem, with various shades of meaning which should be carefully distinguished. Its derivation is from the A.-S. *witan*, 'to know,' so that its primary meaning is (*a*) the knowing power, pure intellect, mental capacity as in this place and in lines 53, 61, 210 and elsewhere; then (*b*) in a slightly wider sense, genius, as in line 657; then (*c*) as a synonym for ingenious or gifted writers, as in line 36; next (*d*) it comes to mean knowledge, learning, or ingenuity, as in 259, 447, 468, 494, 508, particularly 'polite learning,' 652. Next it is a synonym (*e*) for imagination or fancy, as in 292, 590, 717, 722. Then (*f*) it is employed for judgment, as in the couplet 80, 81:

"Some, to whom Heav'n in wit has been profuse,
Want as *much more*, to turn it to its use,"

where it is employed in a double sense, imagination, and the control of imagination, *i.e.* judgment. Lastly, it is employed in the sense in which it was occasionally used in Pope's time and is generally used now: namely, as "a combination of heterogeneous images, the discovery of occult resemblances between things apparently dissimilar," as in line 28.

"In search of wit these lose their common sense,"

and in line 292,

"One glaring Chaos and wild heap of wit.'

For the use of the word in line 297 see the note there.

20. **Most have the seeds of judgment.** Pope quotes Cicero, *de Orat.* III. (ch. l., 195): "Omnes tacito quodam sensu, sine

ulla arte aut ratione, quae sint in artibus ac rationibus, recta et prava dijudicant"; 'All men, by a sort of tacit sense, without any artistic skill or reasoning power, distinguish between what is right and wrong in art and reasoning."

24. **But.** Only.

25. Notice the use of the triplet which Pope employs eight times in the course of the poem. It was introduced, like the Alexandrine, to give variety to the heroic couplet. It was introduced by the Elizabethan poets, and is to be found in Hall, Phaer, and Chapman: used very sparingly by Denham and Cowley, it was first used in excess by Dryden. After the translation of *Homer* Pope very rarely employed it.

26. **maze of schools.** Conflicting sects and systems, which are compared to perplexing labyrinths. *Maze* properly means confusion or perplexity. Skeat traces it to the Scandinavian *masa*, 'to be continually busy at a thing,' and to the Middle English *masen*, 'to confuse or puzzle.' *Amaze* is the same word with the A.-S. intensive prefix.

27. **coxcombs.** Coxcomb is properly a fool or fop, and is a corruption of cock's comb, a cock's crest being symbolic of a swaggering fool. The sense is very badly expressed, the meaning is: And some, whom nature only meant to be fools become conceited fellows. Elwin happily quotes Dryden, *Hind and Panther*, III. 1107:

> "For fools are doubly fools, endeav'ring to be wise."

28. **In search of wit.** See note on line 17.

29. **And then turn Critics.** Parodied from Dryden, *Medal*, 51:

> "The wretch turned loyal in his own defence."

30. **Each burns alike.** In the first edition this couplet ran:

> "Those hate as rivals all that write: and others
> But envy wits as eunuchs envy lovers."

The couplet as it now stands is much more complicated in expression; it may be thus paraphrased: Those who can write burn with the spite of rivals, those who cannot write with the envious spite of impotence. In the 'who' for 'he who,' Pope imitates, as he often does, a common use of the Latin *qui*. Cf. lines 35 and 169: "I know there are, to whose," etc., "There are who judge." So, too, *Prologue to the Satires*, 115: "There are who to my person pay their court." "Who can, or cannot," is of course in apposition to "each." For the sentiment cf. Dryden's *Prologue* to the Second Part of the *Conquest of Granada*:

> "They who write ill, and they who ne'er durst write,
> Turn critics out of mere revenge and spite."

32. **still.** Constantly, always, continually.

34. **If Mævius scribble.** Maevius, who is generally coupled with Bavius, was, like Bavius, a wretched poetaster, contemporary with Virgil and Horace, and would long since have been forgotten had he not been gibbeted by Virgil, *Ecl.* III. 90: "Qui Bavium non odit, amet tua carmina, Maevi." 'May the man who loathes not Bavius love your strains, Maevius'; and by Horace, who in the Tenth *Epode* calls him "olentum," 'stinking,' and curses the ship which is carrying him to Greece.

In Apollo's spite. Apollo was the god of music and poetry. The phrase is from Dryden, Translation of Persius, *Sat.* I. 100:

"Who would be poets in Apollo's spite."

36. **Some have at first for Wits,** etc. This was interpreted at the time as glancing at John Dennis, a well-known critic, with whom Pope was afterwards embroiled in no very reputable controversy. He is referred to by name in line 270, and allusively in line 585. For *Wits* see note on line 17.

38. **neither can.** The 'neither' should properly go with 'wits': it is an illustration of the many grammatical inaccuracies which abound in this poem.

39. **As heavy mules.** There are two points here; the first is that they are neither one thing nor the other, and the second that they are barren.

40. **witling.** The suffix '-ling' expresses diminution. Cf. duckling, gosling, and the like.

41. **half-form'd insects.** This passage was no doubt suggested by Dryden in the Dedication of his Virgil: "You will look on these half lines hereafter as the imperfect products of a hasty muse, like the frogs and serpents on the Nile, part of them kindled into life, and part a lump of unformed, unanimated mud." The grammatical construction, though a little loose, is correct: 'One knows not what to call those half-learned witlings, as numerous in our island as,' etc.

43. **equivocal.** Properly of like sound, so ambiguous, doubtful. Equivocal generation is the production of animals without any certain parentage. Many of the creatures on the Nile were supposed to have originated in this way, formed, it was believed, by the action of the sun upon the slime.

44. **tell,** to count. A.-S. *tellan.*

45. **Or one vain wit's.** The construction is very faulty, and was ridiculed by the author of the *Supplement to the Profound,* quoted by Elwin: "I have often thought that one pert fellow's tongue might tire a hundred pair of attending ears, but I never conceived that it could communicate any lassitude to the tongues of the bystanders before." Pope's meaning is that 'it would tire a hundred ordinary tongues to talk as much as one vain wit.'

47. **noble name.** Note, again, Pope's insistence on the dignity of criticism.

48-50. **Be sure yourself.** An imitation of Horace, *Ars Poet.* 38 *seq.*:

"Sumite materiam vestris, qui scribitis, aequam
Viribus; et versate diu, quid ferre recusent,
Quid valeant humeri."

'Good authors, take a brother bard's advice,
Ponder your subject o'er not once nor twice,
And oft and oft consider, if the weight
You hope to lift be or be not too great.'
(Conington's translation.)

52-9. **Nature to all things ... melt away.** Pope in this passage is commenting on the equilibrium which Nature seems to maintain in man's faculties; if the memory or the purely receptive faculties are too powerful, the understanding or the intellect generally will be proportionately weak; if imagination predominate, the memory will be defective. It is easy to question the soundness of his theory by appealing to particular instances, to show, for example, that Dr. Johnson and Macaulay united extraordinarily tenacious memories with powerful understandings; and that Milton and Dante united marvellous imaginative power with equal power of receptivity or memory, but speaking generally, Pope is right. 'Pretending,' in line 53, means aspiring or ambitious: for 'wit,' see note on line 17.

61. **vast is art,** etc. Suggested by the famous maxim which opens the *Aphorisms* of Hippocrates, ὁ βίος βραχὺς, ἡ δὲ τέχνη μακρὴ, "Life is short but art is long": for 'wit' see note on line 17.

62. **peculiar arts.** From the Latin *peculium*, 'private property,' so what belongs to oneself, particular.

68. **follow Nature.** So Shaftesbury: "Frame taste by the just standard of nature." Bowles remarks that there is some difficulty in determining what is meant by 'Nature' and her 'just standard'; but Pope means by Nature simplicity and sincerity, opposing the term to those metaphysical ideas of nature which had prevailed during the Middle Ages; or more comprehensively the antithesis of what is affected and artificial. His meaning is made more clear by a reference to line 135, "Nature and Homer were, he found, the same."

76. **informing**: moulding, animating. Lat. *informare.*

80. **wit.** See note on line 17.

83. **meant.** From the A.-S. *mænan*, 'to intend': the full construction requires 'for.' Cf. line 27, where there is the same ellipse.

84. **Restrain his fury.** Cf. Longinus, *De Sub.*, sect. II., δεῖ γὰρ αὐτοῖς ὡς κέντρου πολλάκις, οὕτω δὴ καὶ χαλινοῦ, "for as they often require the spur, so also indeed the curb."

85. **The winged courser.** Pegasus, the horse of the Muses, who is fabled to have struck out with his hoof the fountain Hippocrene on Mount Helicon.

86. **gen'rous.** Thoroughbred or high-bred. Lat. *generosus.*

87. **mettle.** Spirit, ardour. It is the same word as 'metal,' and the meaning is derived from the temper of a metal sword blade. There is an exact analogy in the Greek αἰχμή, which means properly the point of a spear, and thence temper, spirit, or disposition.

88. **Those Rules of old.** All canons or rules of criticism are nothing but deductions from the works of great artists, and those works, being inspired by, and exactly true to, nature, are identified with nature. Cf. Dryden's Preface to *Troilus and Cressida*: "If the rules be well considered, we shall find them to be made only to reduce nature to method."

90. **Nature, like liberty.** Till the edition of 1743, 'monarchy' was the reading for 'liberty.' The meaning is: Nature, like liberty, is restrained only by the laws which she herself ordained —a questionable and somewhat unintelligible remark. Longinus seems nearer the mark when he observes (*De Sub.*, section II.), that what curbs nature are the restraints of art.

94. **Parnassus' top.** Parnassus, the mountain sacred to the muses, was in Phocis.

96. **th' immortal prize.** The reference is to the prizes offered at the dramatic competitions at the festival of Dionysus at Athens.

98. **precepts ... giv'n.** A construction answering to the Latin ablative absolute, 'being given.'

105. **Who could not.** See note on line 30.

106. **Against the Poets.** Wakefield quotes some remarks of Dryden in his Dedication to *Ovid* as furnishing the germ of this passage: "Formerly the critics were quite another species of men. They were defenders of poets and commentators on their work. ... Are our auxiliary forces turned our enemies? Are they from our seconds become principals against us?"

108. **'Pothecaries.** For apothecaries, derived from the Low Lat. *apothecarius*, properly 'the keeper of a store-house,' derived in its turn from the Greek ἀποθήκη, 'a store-house.'

109. **Doctor's bills.** Prescriptions.

112. **Some on the leaves.** This passage shows that Pope's contempt for philologists, commentators, *et id genus omne*, did

not date from his own failure as an editor of Shakespeare, as Johnson implies.

117. **explain the meaning**. Cf. the admirable couplet in the *Dunciad*, IV. 251, 252:

"Explain a thing till all men doubt it,
And write about it, Goddess, and about it."

120. **fable**, plot in a play, narrative in an epic.

121-3. With these remarks should be compared what Sainte Beuve says about the questions which a critic should ask himself before he passes judgment on an author, *Nouveaux Lundis*, art. on Chateaubriand.

123. **cavil**, raise captious objections. From Lat. *cavillari*, *cavilla*, 'empty, vain speech.'

124. **Be Homer's works**. Suggested by Horace, *Ars Poet.*, 268, 269:

"Vos exemplaria Graeca
Nocturnâ versate manu, versate diurnâ."

Cf. too Sheffield, *Essay on Poetry*:

"Read Homer once and you can read no more,
For all books else appear so mean and poor;
Verse will seem prose, but still persist to read,
And Homer will be all the books you need."

129. **Mantuan Muse**, Virgil. Publius Vergilius Maro was born at Andes, a small village near Mantua, in Cisalpine Gaul. Dante calls him (*Purgat.* VI. 74) "Mantovano."

131. **A work t' outlast**. Pope was taunted by Dennis with being guilty of a bull in speaking of a work which was to outlast immortality, and altered the lines,

"When first young Maro sung of kings and wars,
Ere warning Phoebus touched his trembling ears";

but afterwards, feeling no doubt that Dennis' objection was hypercritical, he restored, in the last edition, the former reading.

138. **Stagirite**, Aristotle, born at Stagira, which was a town in Thrace, B.C. 384. His extant critical works are the *Poetic* and the *Rhetoric*. The 'i' in Stagira is long, but Pope, following Dryden, shortens it here as elsewhere.

141. **Some beauties**. Elwin aptly quotes Rapin, *Collected Works*, Vol. II., p. 173; English translation, 'There are no precepts to teach the hidden graces and all that secret power of poetry which passes to the heart.'

150. **Pegasus**, see note on l 86.

152. **brave disorder**. Cf. Soame and Dryden of the ode in the translation of Boileau's *Art of Poetry* (quoted by Elwin):

"And by a brave disorder shows her art."

Cf. too Pope himself, of Homer, in the *Temple of Fame*:

"And here and there disclosed a brave neglect."

159. **gloriously offend**, an oxymoron transferred apparently from Dryden's *Aurungzebe*, Act IV.:

"Mean soul, and dar'st not gloriously offend."

For 'wits,' see note on l. 17.

161. **their**, their own.

167. **remorse**, pity, the common meaning of the word in our old writers.

169. **there are, to whose**. See note on l. 30.

170. **faults**. Not a false rhyme with 'thoughts,' for the 'l' was not sounded before nor in Pope's time.

172-4. **Which ... But**, suggested by Horace, *Ars Poetica*, 361-3:

"Ut pictura, poesis erit; quae, si propius stes,
Te capiat magis, et quaedam, si longius abstes;
Haec amat obscurum, volet haec sub luce videri."

'It is with a poem as with a picture. This attracts you the more the closer you stand to it; another the further you stand from it. One courts obscurity; this will prefer to be seen in a full light.'

180. **Homer nods**. Cf. Horace, *Ars Poet.*, 359:

"Indignor quandoque bonus dormitat Homerus."

'I take it ill whenever dear old Homer nods.'

Pope may have designed this to glance at Lord Roscommon, who writes in his *Essay on Translated Verse*, speaking of Homer's heroes:

"Whose railing heroes and whose wounded gods
Make some suspect he snores as well as nods."

182. **Above the reach**. This line is transferred literally from Roscommon's *Epilogue to Alexander the Great*.

sacrilegious. Profane or impious, from *sacra legere*, 'to gather up sacred things.'

183. **Secure from flames**. The allusions in this couplet are, according to Warburton, to the destruction of the Alexandrine and Palatine libraries by fire; the fiercer rage of Zoilus and Maevius and their followers against wit; the irruption of the barbarians into the Empire; and the long reign of ignorance and superstition in the cloisters.

184. **all-involving**, all-covering or all-investing.

186. **consenting Pæans**. A paean was properly a hymn to the Healing God, Apollo; the Greek παιάν; 'consenting,' from *consentire*, is sympathetic.

189. **Hail, Bards.** This noble passage is a fitting climax to the first stage of the poem. The first line is a translation of Virgil's

"Magnanimi heroes! nati melioribus annis."

Aen. VI. 649.

194. **must not yet.** The force of 'must' will be best understood by an account of its etymology. The verb from which it is derived, *motan*, is so defective that it was used only in the present tense of the Middle English form *mot, moote*, 'I am able,' 'I can,' the preterite of which is *moste*, 'I could,' 'I might,' 'I ought'; and so the idea of compulsion was associated with it. Cf. the German *müssen*. Sometimes, however, it recurs to its original meaning, as here: 'worlds that are not able to be found—cannot yet be found.' Pope's line, as Wakefield notes, is an imitation of a line in Cowley's *Davideis*, ii. 833:

"And reach to worlds that must not yet be found."

II.

203. **bias.** An inclination towards one side, a slope. French, *biais*, 'a slant,' 'slope.' Its common application is to the bulge on a bowling ball, or the curved course taken by the ball.

204. **Pride.** Used in the sense of 'arrogant vanity,' the χαυνότης of Aristotle. For the idea cf. *Essay on Man*, epist. II. 285-6.

"Each want of happiness by hope supplied,
And each vacuity of sense by pride;
These build as fast as knowledge can destroy."

206. **For as in bodies.** Pope's physiology here is all nonsense, and the language is so confused that he appears to assign blood and spirits to souls as well as to bodies.

214. **Make use of ev'ry ... foe.** A friend visiting Archbishop Tillotson observed in his library a shelf of books of different forms and sizes, but all very richly bound and finely gilt and lettered. "Those," said the archbishop, "are my own personal friends, and, which is more, whom I have myself made such (for they meant to be my enemies) by the use I have made of those hints which their malice hath suggested to me, and from which I have received more profit than from the advice of my best and most cordial friends; and, therefore, you see I have rewarded them accordingly."

216. **Pierian spring.** Hippocrene. The Muses were called Pierides, probably from Pieria, near Mount Olympus, where they were first worshipped. There was a legend that the nine daughters of Pierus challenged the Muses to sing on Mount

Helicon; and the mountain was so ravished with the sound of the Muses' songs that it was rising gradually to heaven, till Pegasus stopt its ascent by giving it a kick, and from this kick arose Hippocrene, the inspiring well of the Muses.

216. The hint for this famous passage was, no doubt, derived from Bacon's *Essay of Atheism*: "It is true that a little philosophy inclineth man's mind to Atheism, but depth in philosophy bringeth men's minds about to religion."

225. **So pleas'd at first.** This noble simile is pronounced by Dr. Johnson to be "perhaps the best that English poetry can show. A simile, to be perfect," he continues, "must both illustrate and ennoble the subject, must show it to the understanding in a clearer view, and display it to the fancy with greater dignity, but either of these qualities may be sufficient to recommend it. ... The simile of the Alps has no useless parts, yet affords a striking picture by itself: it makes the foregoing position better understood, and enables it to take faster hold on the attention; it assists the apprehension and elevates the fancy" (*Life of Pope*). It detracts very little from Pope's credit that he may have found the germ of the simile in Drummond of Hawthornden, *An Hymn of the Fairest Fair*, in *Flowers of Zion*. The lines resembling Pope's may be compared:

> "Ah! as a pilgrim who the Alps doth pass
> . . . .
> When he some heaps of hills hath overwent
> Begins to think on rest, his journey spent,
> Till mounting some tall mountain he doth find
> More heights before him than he left behind."

With the lesson Pope here teaches may be compared what the great civil lawyer Cujas said of his studies of the law: that at the end of the first ten years he thought he knew all that could be known; at the end of the next decade he felt painfully that he knew very little; the end of the third decade enabled him to realize the extent of his ignorance.

233-4. **A perfect Judge.** This is very badly expressed, but the meaning is clear: A perfect judge will endeavour to put himself in the position of the author whom he is criticising, enter into his spirit, and approach him sympathetically. But Pope's illustrative quotation from Quintilian, which it is not necessary to transcribe, would seem to imply that he meant that a critic should take as much trouble in judging a book as the author took in composing it.

238. **Wit.** See note on l. 17.

239. **But in such lays.** In the case of. 'In' is often used in this sense in Latin. With these lines may be compared Longinus, *De Sub.* XXXIII.

244. **peculiar.** See note on l. 62.

247, 248. **well-proportion'd dome.** The reference is either to the Pantheon at Rome or to St. Peter's.

251. **appear.** This is a mistake in grammar, as the nominatives are in the singular and 'or' is a disjunctive.

256. **none** ... **they.** As 'none' is properly singular, being simply a contraction for *no one*, it should not go with a plural verb. But it is commonly used with plural verbs, and usage in all languages carries as much authority as grammar.

258. **trivial.** From Lat. *trivialis*, properly what is found at a *trivium*, a place where three roads meet. So *trite*, 'commonplace.' With this couplet may be compared the passage which suggested it—Horace, *Ars Poetica*, 351, 352:

> "Verum ubi plura nitent in carmine, non ego paucis
> Offendar maculis."

'But when the shining passages predominate in a poem, I shall not take offence at a few blemishes.'

261. **verbal**, minutely exact in words. In Shakespeare the word is used for verbose, or wordy.

261. **Lays** down, the expression in the original is justly censured by Warton as very objectionable.

262. **For not to know.** From Quintilian I.: "Ex quo mihi inter virtutes grammatici habebitur aliqua nescire." 'Hence I shall reckon among the virtues of a humanist to be ignorant of some things.'

263-6. Most critics judge by parts and not by the whole. They lay stress on those subordinate parts of a poet's work which their own taste inclines them to appreciate and by these they judge of the whole work; for these practically represent to them the whole work. They talk of principles, but are really guided by their own preferences. Cf. Lessing's remarks in the Preface to his *Laocoon*.

267. **La Mancha's Knight,** Don Quixote. The passage which follows is not taken from Cervantes' work, but from a work purporting to be the Second Part of *Don Quixote*, written, to the great annoyance of Cervantes, by some one who called himself Don Alonzo Fernandez de Avellanada. Mr. Watts in his *Life of Cervantes* conjectures that this was a name assumed by Lope de Vega. The work was published in 1614. It was afterwards translated and remodelled by Le Sage. The passage referred to by Pope is as follows: "I am satisfied you'll compass your design," said the scholar, "provided you omit the combat in the lists." "Let him have a care of that," said Don Quixote interrupting him; "that is the best part of the plot." "But, sir," quoth the Bachelor, "if you would have me adhere to

Aristotle's rules, I must omit the combat." "Aristotle," replied the knight, "I grant was a man of some parts; but his capacity was not unbounded: and give me leave to tell you, his authority does not extend over combats in the list, which are far above his narrow rules. Would you suffer the chaste Queen of Bohemia to perish? For how can you clear her innocence? Believe me, combat is the most honourable method you can pursue, and besides, it will add such grace to your play, that all the rules in the universe must not stand in competition with it. "Well, Sir Knight," replied the Bachelor, "for your sake and for the honour of chivalry I will not leave out the combat, and that it may appear the more glorious all the land of Bohemia shall be present at it, from the princes of the blood, to the very footmen. But still one difficulty remains, which is that our common theatres are not large enough for it." "There must be one erected on purpose," answered the Knight, "and, in a word, rather than leave out the combat the play had better be acted in a field or plain."

270. **Dennis ... Grecian stage.** John Dennis (1657 to 1733-4) is now chiefly remembered as the butt of Pope's satire, but he was a man of no contemptible gifts and attainments. He was the author of several plays and operas and of voluminous critical writings, and both Dryden and Congreve had, at one time at least, a very high opinion of him. The best of his writings are his *Original Letters, Familiar, Moral, and Critical.* He came into collision with Pope after the appearance of the present poem, and the hostility between them, says Johnson, "though suspended for a short time was never appeased." He attacked the *Rape of the Lock,* and then ran amuck on Addison's *Cato.* This elicited from Pope a disgusting pamphlet, which was more disgraceful to its author than to its subject. Pope has attacked him in the *Prologue to the Satires* and in the *Dunciad*, and contributed a sarcastic Prologue to the play acted for poor Dennis' benefit in December, 1733. The reference to the Grecian stage is probably to the remarks of Dennis on this subject in his *Advancement and Reformation of Modern Poetry,* published in 1701.

271. **sots,** fools or blockheads. Fr. *sot.* The etymology is very doubtful.

273. **nice,** discriminating.

280. **Stagirite.** See note on l. 138.

276. **unities.** The unities of action, time, and place were the deductions of the French critics from Aristotle's *Poetics,* and from the Greek tragedies. They were first formulated by Corneille in his three essays, published in 1659, and after that became the battle-ground of successive generations of critics. Stated briefly, the unity of action is the elimination of every-

thing which does not conduce directly to the catastrophe; the unity of time prescribes a revolution of the sun as the time to be comprised in the evolution of the plot; the unity of place, that the scene must not change. For an admirable discussion of the correctness and incorrectness of this doctrine, see Schlegel, *Lectures on Dramatic Literature*, Lectures XVII. and XVIII. and Twining's Dissertation in his translation of Aristotle's *Poetics*, Vol. I., pp. 337-41.

277. **were**: the subjunctive mood, 'would be.'

278. **lists**: the grounds enclosed for a tournament. Lat. *licium*, 'a thread,' a strip of silk or cloth marking the boundary.

286. **Curious not knowing**. From Petronius, as Pope himself noted, "Non quidem doctus sed curiosus."

289. **Conceit**. Conceit properly means a conception, notion, or idea, being derived from the Lat. *concipio, conceptum*; then it was applied to an odd or fantastic notion, then to an over-estimation of oneself, the sense it generally bears now. Pope uses it in the second sense.

292. **Chaos**. Properly an empty, gaping space. Greek χάος, from χάσκειν, 'to yawn'; then it got applied to matter—Ovid's "rudis indigestaque moles," and Milton's "matter unformed and void," confusion and disorder. For 'wit' see note on l. 17.

297, 298. **True Wit is Nature**. The key to the meaning of this somewhat obscure couplet is to be found partly in Dryden's Preface to the *State of Innocence*. "The definition of wit which has been so often attempted, and ever unsuccessfully, by many poets, is only this, that it is a propriety of thoughts and words," and partly in Boileau, who apparently suggested it: "Qu'est-ce qu'une pensée neuve, brillante, extraordinaire? Ce n'est point, comme se le persuadent les ignorants, une pensée que personne n'a jamais eu, ni dû avoir. C'est au contraire une pensée qui a dû venir à tout le monde, et que quelqu'un s'avise le premier d'exprimer. Un bon mot n'est bon mot qu'en ce qu'il dit une chose que chacun pensoit, et qu'il la dit d'une manière vive, fine et nouvelle." What Pope means, then, is this, that as false wit perverts or distorts nature, by refracting it into unnatural and fantastic shapes, as a kaleidoscope does, so true wit is the power of representing nature not merely with propriety but in such a way that her native charms are heightened in the presentment. The second line is really only a repetition, slightly extended, of the idea in the first. Cf. lines 311-9, which form a good commentary on this couplet. Cf. also Buckingham, *Essay on Poetry*, 270, 271, where distinguishing between 'humour' and 'wit,' he says:

> "Humour is all; wit should be only brought
> To turn agreeably some proper thought.

299. **Something, whose truth.** This is very elliptically expressed. It may perhaps be explained in two ways, *i.e.* taking whose truth = the truth of which, as the objective after find, so 'the truth of which we convinced (of that truth) find at first sight'; or 'of whose truth we find (ourselves) convinced at first sight.' Possibly it is a mixture of the two constructions. With these remarks of Pope compare Addison: "Wit and fine writing do not consist so much in advancing things that are new as in giving things that are known an agreeable turn. It is impossible for us, who live in the later ages of the world, to make observations in criticism, morality, or in any art or science which have not been touched upon by others. We have little else left us but to represent the commonsense of mankind in more strong, more beautiful, or more uncommon lights."—*Spectator*, No. 253.

301, 302. **light, ... wit.** There are many faulty rhymes in the poem, but there are few as bad as this. For 'wit' see note on l. 17.

303. **does 'em good.** A strange vulgarism, employed perhaps to mark the somewhat colloquial tone of the poem.

308. **take upon content.** Take upon trust. Elwin quotes what Rymer says of the actor Hart, "What he delivers every one takes upon content."

311. **prismatic glass.** "A prism is a glass bounded with two equal and parallel triangular ends and three plain and well polished sides, which meet in three parallel lines, running from the three angles of one end to the three angles of the other end" (Newton's definition, quoted by Johnson).

319. **decent,** becoming. Lat. *decens.*

320. **conceit,** here conception. See note on l. 289.

322. **sort.** Be of the same class with, so harmonize.

324. **some by old words ... pretence.** Many years after Pope, Gifford in his *Baviad,* ridiculed those who

> "For *ekes* and *algates* only deign to seek
> And live upon a *whilom* for a week."

made pretence, lay claim to.

328. **Fungoso,** a character in Ben Jonson's *Every Man out of his Humour.* He is described in the *dramatis personae* as "a student, one that has revelled in his time, and follows the fashion afar off, as a spy."

329. **These sparks.** Johnson defines a spark as a lively, showy, splendid, gay man, adding "it is commonly used in contempt."

332. **doublets.** This, formerly an outer garment with sleeves and sometimes skirts, became, about the middle of the seventeenth

century, an inner garment, developing at last into the modern waistcoat.

334. **fantastic.** The word derived directly from the Greek φαντασία, 'a making visible,' 'imagination,' hence our fantasy, fancy, etc. It gradually came to mean what is purely imaginary, so whimsical or odd.

341. **Parnassus.** See note to l. 94.

344. **These equal syllables.** Note how admirably these and the following verses imitate and illustrate what they satirize.

346. **expletives**, from the Latin *explere*, 'to fill up,' denote small superfluous words not needed by the sense, but introduced for the purpose of emphasis or rhythm.

347. **And ten low words.** Warburton notices that this is borrowed from a passage in Dryden's *Essay of Dramatic Poesy*: "He creeps along with ten little words in every line, and helps out his numbers with *for*, *to*, and *unto*, and all the petty expletives he can find."

356. **Alexandrine.** An Alexandrine is a verse of six iambic feet and twelve or thirteen syllables in English, as is illustrated by the next line. The name is commonly derived from a poem of the twelfth century dealing with Alexander the Great and his fabulous adventures, and entitled, *Alexandriade, ou Chanson de Geste D'Alexandre le grand*, the first poem written in this measure. It was commenced by Lambert le Court, and continued by Alexandre de Bernay, known also as Alexandre de Paris, from whose name and not from the poem, according to some authorities, the name is derived.

361. **Denham...Waller.** Sir John Denham (1615-1668) is chiefly celebrated as the author of *Cooper's Hill*, a poem ridiculously over-praised by his contemporaries and immediate successors. Thus Dryden, in the *Essay of Dramatic Poesy*, speaks of Denham's poetry as "majestic and correct"; and Pope, in *Windsor Forest*, 267, informs us that

"On Cooper's Hill eternal wreaths shall blow,"

and in the same poem, line 271, calls him, echoing Dryden, 'majestic Denham.' He was certainly one of the leaders of the 'critical school,' and is fairly entitled to the praise of writing in a terse and smooth style. His four lines on the Thames are deservedly celebrated:

"O could I flow like thee, and make thy stream
My great example, as it is my theme;
Tho' deep yet clear, tho' gentle, yet not dull,
Strong without rage, without o'erflowing full."

Edmund Waller (1605-1687). The epithet 'sweet,' applied to Waller's verses, is more intelligible than the epithet applied to

Denham's. Some of Waller's poems, such as the popular lyric, "Go, lovely rose," and the verses on old age, are never likely to be forgotten. His "Panegyric upon the Lord Protector" is not unworthy of the subject. Historically he is of great importance in English poetry; and though Dryden goes too far when he says in his preface to the *Rival Ladies*, that "the excellence and dignity of rhyme were never fully known till Mr. Waller taught it, he first made writing easily an art," yet he indicates truly Waller's position: he was, like Denham, one of the fathers of the 'critical school.' Waller's verse is polished and musical, his diction neat, terse, and felicitous.

365. **The sound must seem.** In the verses which follow, Pope has imitated closely a passage in the third book of Vida's *Poetica* (see Introduction). Johnson's remarks in his *Life of Pope* on this passage, on Pope's attempts at onomatopoeia, or making the sound an echo to the sense, should be read.

370. **When Ajax strives.** Ajax, the son of Telamon, was one of the giants in the army of the Greeks at Troy. He twice hurls stones in the *Iliad*: see *Iliad*, VII. 268-71 and *Iliad*, XII. 380-5.

372. **swift Camilla.** Camilla, the warrior maiden of the Volsciani, is thus described by Virgil, *Aen.* VII. 808-11, in lines which Pope had in his mind when writing this passage.

> "Illa vel intactae segetis per summa volaret
> Gramina, nec teneras cursu laesisset aristas;
> Vel mare per medium, fluctu suspensa tumenti,
> Ferret iter, celeres nec tingueret aequore plantas."

'She over the tops of the unsickled corn might have flitted and have harmed not in her course the tender ears, or through the midst of the sea have made her way, poised on the heaving wave, and not wetted her swift soles.'

374. **Timotheus.** In these lines the reference is to Dryden's *Alexander's Feast*, where the poet represents the strains of Timotheus having these various effects on Alexander. The student should turn to this magnificent Ode, and Pope's lines will be readily intelligible.

376. **son of Libyan Jove.** This refers to the famous legend that Alexander the Great was the son of Zeus Ammon, a Libyan deity, whose oracle was in the oasis of Ammonium in the Libyan desert. In the prologue to the *Satires*, line 117, Pope speaks of him as "Ammon's great son."

384. **is Dryden now,** that is, the power and charm which Timotheus had as a musician, Dryden has as a poet. Dryden was the poetical father of Pope. "I learned versification wholly from Dryden's works, who had improved it much beyond any of our former poets" (Pope, in Spence's *Anecdotes*, Malone's Edit., p. 114). As Dryden, born in 1631, died in May, 1700, Pope had

not completed his twelfth year when he lost his master, whom, however, he saw once.

391. **fools admire.** Exactly the Latin *admirari*, 'to feel astonishment.' Cf. Hor. *Epistles*, I. vi. 1, 2:

" Nil admirari prope res est una, Numici,
Solaque, quae possit facere et servare beatum,"

which Creech turned:

" Not to admire is all the art I know
To make men happy and to keep them so,"

and this version Pope sarcastically adopted in his *Imitation* of that Epistle, where it stands as the opening couplet. It is curious that Pope should have been indebted to Creech for the very phrase, 'fools admire.'

Approve means 'to put to the test,' 'prove by trial.'

394. **Some foreign writers.** In this and the following line Pope refers to the controversy about the relative value and importance of the ancient and the modern writers, which, originating in France towards the end of the seventeenth century, spread to England and led to the famous Phalaris controversy, and to the composition of Swift's satire, the *Battle of the Books*. For an account of this see Macaulay's *Essay on Sir William Temple* and De Quincey's *Essay on Bentley*.

397. **To one small sect.** This gave great offence to the Roman Catholics, whose sentiments Pope literally expressed, though with a sarcastic turn. Pope's remarks in a letter to his friend Caryll are interesting. "Nothing has been so much a scarecrow to our opponents as that too peremptory and uncharitable assertion of an utter impossibility of salvation to all but ourselves. I own to you I was glad of any opportunity to express my dislike of so shocking a sentiment as those of the religion I profess are commonly charged with, and I hoped a slight insinuation, introduced by a casual similitude only, could never have given offence."

398. **Meanly they seek.** The Roman Catholics taking exception to this couplet also, Pope ingeniously explained that the 'they' referred to 'Some' in l. 394.

400. **sublimes.** This was a term for an operation in alchemy whereby the subtler parts were separated from the grosser, and so the word came to mean 'to purify.'

403. **Enlights.** For enlightens; a very rare form of the word which Wakefield thinks was coined by Pope, but the *Century Dictionary* shows that it is to be found in Cowley:

" The wisest king refined all pleasures quite,
Till wisdom from above did him enlight."

Mistress Wisdom.

415. **joins with Quality**. Joins with people of rank. The term was used both in an abstract and a concrete sense: 'a person of quality' was a person of rank; 'the quality' were people of rank. So Addison in the *Guardian*, quoted by Johnson: "I shall appear at the masquerade dressed up in my feathers, that the quality may see how pretty they will look." It is still occasionally used, but it is now a vulgarism.

418. **madrigal**. A pure Italian word *madrigale*, pl. *madrigali*, explained by Florio as 'short songs or ditties,' generally of a pastoral kind, a shepherd's song, hence its derivation from *mandriale*, 'a herdsman' or 'drover.'

419. **hackney**. Properly a horse let out for hire, so a mercenary drudge: *hack* is another form.

425. **singular**, standing alone; have something not common with others; so, almost, independent.

428. **Schismatics**, properly splitters-off; from σχίζειν, 'to split,' so dissentients. The accent is on the antepenultimate.

429. **wit**. See note on l. 17.

434. **like towns unfortify'd**. The sense is clear, but the grammatical construction is slipshod and confused. Towns unfortified frequently change sides, but not as weak heads do, hovering between sense and nonsense.

441. **Sentences**. The reference is to the *Book of Sentences* compiled by Peter Lombard, Bishop of Paris, in 1159, which was intended to be, and really became, the manual of the schools. Thomas Aquinas wrote a commentary on it.

444. **Scotists and Thomists**. The Scotists were the followers of Duns Scotus, "the subtle doctor," who was born about 1260, became Professor of Theology at Oxford in 1301, and died in or about 1308. The Thomists were the followers of Thomas Aquinas, a Neapolitan, the "angelic doctor"; he was born about 1227, became a scholar of Albert the Great; lectured at Cologne and Paris, and died in 1274. "The war of Scotists and Thomists long divided the schools," says Milman, "not the less fierce from the utter darkness in which it was enveloped." For an account of it see Milman's *Hist. of Latin Christianity*, Vol. IX., ch. iii.

445. **Duck-lane**. "A place, where old and second-hand books were sold formerly, near Smithfield" (Pope's note); so Swift, Verses on his own death:

"Some country squire to Lintot goes,
Inquires for Swift in verse and prose.
Says Lintot, 'I have heard the name,
He died a year ago'—'The same.'
He searches all the shop in vain:
'Sir, you may find them in Duck-lane.'"

447. **modes.** Fashions. A man of mode was the common expression for a man of fashion. Cf. the French *mode*, meaning the same thing, and probably the origin of the term.

449. **The current folly proves.** The test of an author's reputation, or in other words, of what constitutes his reputation, *i.e.* his wit, is popularity, and as a large proportion of those whose opinions constitute popularity are fools, current folly is practically the test of the wit of the moment. The passage may be compared with the passage in Shakespeare's *Troilus and Cressida*, III. iii.:

"No man is the lord of any thing,
Though in and of him there be much consisting,
Till he communicate his parts to others;
Nor doth he of himself know them for aught
Till he behold them formed in th' applause
Where they are extended."

458-9. **Pride, Malice, ... In various shapes.** The 'parsons' who attacked Dryden were the Rev. Jeremy Collier in his *Short View of the Profaneness and Immorality of the English Stage*, and the Rev. Luke Milbourn in his *Notes on Dryden's Virgil*, 1698. See Johnson's life of Dryden and also Scott's. The 'beaus' were probably George Villiers, Duke of Buckingham, who as one of the authors of the *Rehearsal*, 1671, held Dryden up to ridicule as Bayes. Also John Wilmot, Earl of Rochester, who attacked him in his *Allusion to the Tenth Satire of Horace*, and hired some bravos to waylay and cudgel him because of some verses in Sheffield's *Essay on Satire*, attributed to Dryden, in which Rochester had been satirized. Among the 'critics' may be numbered Thomas Shadwell, the subject of Dryden's Mac Flecknoe, who attacked Dryden in *The Medal of John Bayes* and *Dryden's Satire to his Muse.* Elkanah Settle, who had assailed him in his *Absalom Senior*, and Sir Richard Blackmore, who had spoken very severely of him in a *Satire against Wit.*

463. **Blackmores ... Milbourns.** Sir Richard Blackmore was physician to William III. and to Queen Anne, and was a voluminous writer both in verse and prose. The works by which he was most known were *The Creation*, a didactic poem in seven books, which was highly praised both by Addison and by Dr. Johnson, an epic poem on King Alfred in twelve books, and a sacred poem called *The Redeemer*. He died in 1729, and his biography has been written by Dr. Johnson in the *Lives of the Poets.* Of Luke Milbourn little more is known than the fact that he was educated at Cambridge, held preferments in the church, and died in 1720. He was satirized by Dryden, and is one of the heroes of the *Dunciad.* Of his strictures on Dryden's *Virgil* Dr. Johnson has given a specimen which he might just as well have spared us.

465. **Zoilus.** It is uncertain when Zoilus lived: he is said to have been a native of Amphipolis, and to have migrated to Alexandria during the reign of Ptolemy Philadelphus (born B.C. 309, died B.C. 247). But this is doubtful: he was famous for his attack on Homer, and was nicknamed 'Ὁμηρομάστιξ, 'the scourge of Homer.' Dionysius of Halicarnassus speaks of him with respect, and classes him among critics of the highest rank.

468. **Wit.** See note on line 17.

479. **Patriarch-wits.** Referring to the long lives of the Patriarchs.

483. **such as Chaucer is**, etc. True, in a very different sense to the sense intended by Pope, who meant, of course, that Dryden would come to be as obsolete as Chaucer. As a matter of fact Chaucer is now more popular than Dryden. From the Elizabethan age downward, there seems to have been an impression that nothing written in English would last, and that was one of the reasons why it was usual to have important works translated into Latin. So Waller *Of English Verse*:

> " Poets that lasting marble seek
> Must carve in Latin or in Greek;
> We write in sand: our language grows,
> And like the tide our work o'erflows."

484. **So when the faithful pencil.** "Nothing," says Warton, commenting on these lines, "was ever more happily expressed on the subject of painting, a subject of which Pope always speaks *con amore.*" Cf. Pope's *Epistle to Jervas.* Pope, like Euripides, was himself an amateur painter. Some of his paintings are extant —a head of Betterton painted by him was in Lord Mansfield's possession. In the beautiful passage in the text he has drawn on the equally beautiful lines which close Dryden's *Epistle to Sir Godfrey Kneller*:

> " More cannot be by mortal art exprest,
> But venerable age shall add the rest;
> For Time shall with his ready pencil stand,
> Retouch your figures with his ripening hand,
> Mellow your colours and embrown the teint,
> Add every grace which time alone can grant;
> To future ages shall your fame convey,
> And give more beauties than he takes away."

493. **And all the bright.** An echo of Addison (*Account of the Greatest English Poets*, 31):

> " And all the pleasing landscape fades away."

495. **Atones not for.** Atones, a compound of *at* and *one*, properly means 'to set at one,' 'to reconcile.' So to bring into harmony or accord, and so 'to make reparation,' 'to compensate.'

501. **The owner's wife.** That is, the wife of the owner of the wit.

503. **The more we give.** The more we give, the more people expect from us.

506, 507. The vicious fear it because they fear its scourge as satire; the virtuous shun it because of its frequent abuse and perversion in the hands of its possessors; fools hate it because they envy those who have it, or because they dread its lash. Why it is 'undone by knaves' is well explained by Warburton: "The poet would insinuate a common but shameful truth, that men in power, if they got power by illiberal arts, generally left Wit and Science to starve." The couplet seems to be a parody of a couplet from the lines on Death in the Third Canto of Garth's *Dispensary*, 230, 231:

"'Tis what the guilty fear, the pious crave,
Sought by the wretch, and vanquish'd by the brave.

509. **commence its foe.** Begin to be its foe. French *commencer.*

511. **endeavour'd well.** This verb grew out of the Middle English phrase, 'to do his devoir' or duty. So Chaucer, *Knight's Tale*, 1600: "Doth now your devoir," 'Do your duty.' So Dr. Johnson, *Preface to Dictionary*: "I deliver it to the world with the spirit of a man that has *endeavoured well.*"

514. **Parnassus' ... crown.** See note on line 94. The repetition of the word is an instance of carelessness rare indeed with Pope.

518, 519. That is, all the unsuccessful authors maligned the successful. The successful authors, as Elwin pertinently remarks, never said anything so slanderous.

521. **sacred lust.** That is, accursed; an imitation of the Latin use of the word, suggested, as Pope notes, by Virgil, *Aen.* III. 56, 57.

"Quid non mortalia pectora cogis,
Auri sacra fames?"

522. **Ah ne'er so dire.** Again from Virgil, *Georg.* I. 37:

"Nec tibi regnandi veniat tam dira cupido."

527. **spleen** (Greek σπλήν). Properly a gland above the kidney, supposed by the ancients to be the seat of anger, ill-humour, and melancholy.

528. **provoking.** In the Latin sense 'calling forth,' 'challenging'—*pro* and *vocare*, 'to call forth.'

529. **flagitious.** From the Latin *flagitiosus*, 'shameful,' 'infamous.'

530. **No pardon.** So Roscommon, *Art of Translating Verse*, in a couplet often erroneously attributed to Pope:

"Immodest words admit of no defence,
For want of decency is want of sense."

536. **an easy Monarch's care.** The reference is to Charles II. Sir Walter Scott once quoted, in conversation, a stanza, from one of the broadsheets of the time, attributed to Buckingham:

> "Here's Lauderdale the pretty,
> And Monmouth the witty,
> And Fraser the learned physician;
> Here's the Duke for a jest,
> And, to crown all the rest,
> Here's Charles for a great politician";

the point being the elaborate impropriety of the attributes assigned to each.

538, 539. **Jilts rul'd the state ... Lords had wit.** The jilts were the various mistresses of Charles; the statesmen who wrote farces were George Villiers, Duke of Buckingham, part author of the *Rehearsal*, one of the Cabal; Sir George Etheridge, author of the *The Comical Revenge*, *She Would if she Could*, and the *Man of Mode*, an ambassador and British plenipotentiary at Ratisbon. The wits who had pensions were certainly less numerous than the wits who had not; perhaps the list does not extend further than St. Evremond. The young lords who had wit have been enumerated by Dennis: "Villiers, Duke of Buckingham; the Earl of Mulgrave; Lord Buckhurst, afterwards Earl of Dorset; the Marquis of Halifax; the Earl of Rochester; Lord Vaughan, and several others."

541. **Mask.** Or masque, a word from the Arabic, properly denoting a covering for the face, and then by easy deduction a person who wore a mask, and an assembly or entertainment where such masks were worn.

542. **modest fan.** As in Charles II.'s reign it became fashionable for ladies to wear masks, a custom attributed by Cibber and Evelyn to the gross immorality and obscenity of the dramas, which no decent woman could witness or listen to with uncovered face, fans went out of use.

543. **at what they blush'd.** 'At that which they blushed at before': a most awkward ellipse.

Between this verse and the following couplet Pope inserted two lines which were afterwards cancelled:

> "Then first the Belgian morals were extoll'd,
> We their religion had, and they our gold."

adding as his reason for omitting them, that they "contained a national reflection, which in his stricter judgment he could not but disapprove, on any people whatever."

545. **bold Socinus.** Laelius Socinus was born at Sienna in 1525, and died at Zurich in 1562, leaving to his more celebrated nephew, Faustus Socinus, born at Sienna, 1539, died near Cracow

in 1604, the task of reducing to a system the tenets which they held. They were the leaders of the sect known as Unitarians, who were opposed to the Catholic Christians in rejecting the doctrine of the Trinity, in denying the divinity of Christ and all that immediately depended on belief in that divinity, the atonement, and the like: they rejected also the doctrine of original sin, of eternal punishment, and the existence of Satan. A common charge against the Latitudinarian school was that they were Socianians.

546. **unbelieving priests.** The particular person glanced at here is supposed to be Gilbert Burnet, Bishop of Sarum, who had been severely attacked by Dryden in the Third Part of the *Hind and Panther*, and who was the most prominent leader of the Latitudinarian school. Pope, as a Roman Catholic, would naturally not regard this school with much favour.

547. **And taught more pleasant.** Jortin, in a note quoted by Elwin, says: "In this line Pope had Kennet in view, who was accused of having said, in a funeral sermon on some nobleman, that converted sinners, if they were men of parts, repented more speedily and effectually than dull rascals": surely a very sensible remark. The Kennet referred to was Dr. White Kennet (1660-1728), Bishop of Peterborough.

550. **their sacred satire.** Cf. the couplet in *Moral Essays*, Epist. IV. 149, 150:

"To rest the cushion and soft Dean invite,
Who never mentions Hell to ears polite,"

and Pope's note to this passage. "This is a fact: a reverend Dean, preaching at Court, threatened the sinner with punishment in 'a place which he thought it not decent to name in so polite an assembly.'"

551. **Vice admir'd.** Wondered—the Latin sense of the term, frequent in our old authors. So Milton, *Par. Lost*, II. 277, 278:

"Th' undaunted fiend, what this might be, *admired*,
Admir'd, not feared."

So again in Bk. I. 690, 691:

"Let none *admire*
That riches grow in hell."

See too note on line 391.

552. **Wit's Titans.** The Titans were the sons and daughters of Uranus and Gê, and after attempting to scale Heaven and depose Zeus, they were overcome and hurled down to Tartarus.

553. **licens'd blasphemies.** Pope may here be referring to the Deistical writers, Toland, Tindal, Collins, and others who were very prominent at the end of the seventeenth and during

the course of the eighteenth centuries. Cf. the reference in the *Dunciad*, II. 399:

> "Toland and Tindal prompt at priests to jeer,
> Yet silent bow'd to *Christ's no kingdom here*,"

a sarcastic allusion to Bishop Hoadley's famous Latitudinarian sermon.

556. **scandalously nice.** Malignantly discriminating.

557. **mistake ... into vice.** Awkwardly expressed, but meaning: 'misrepresent him for the sake of perverting his meaning into something vicious.'

559. **all looks yellow.** Wakefield appositely quotes Lucretius, IV. 333:

> "Lurida praeterea fiunt, quaecunque tuentur
> Arquati."

'Again whatever the jaundiced gaze on becomes a greenish yellow.'

Jaundice is from the French *jaunisse*; yellowness from *jaune*, 'yellow.'

III.

564, 565. That all may allow not simply what is due to your sense, but seek your friendship also.

567. **speak, tho' sure.** Like the Greeks "qui amant omnia dubitantius loqui." In the first edition Pope wrote:

> 'Speak when you're sure, yet speak with diffidence,'

and on Dennis suggesting that a man, when sure, should speak "with a modest assurance," Pope wrote on the margin of his manuscript, "Dennis p. 21, Alter the inconsistency." Like Tillotson he profited from his enemies.

571-7. The young student would do well to take these admirable lines to heart: if followed, they would prove a royal road to what most men arrive at by very circuitous and sometimes painful paths.

577. **That,** *i.e.* good-breeding.

585. **Appius reddens ... tapestry.** The allusion is to Dennis. See note on line 270. But there is a nice propriety in the picture which might easily be missed. 'Reddens' refers to Dennis' sensitively irritable disposition. Pope calls him a "furious old critic." The stare was one of his characteristics. There is a passage quoted by Elwin from Sir Richard Steele in which Dennis is thus described, "He starts, stares, and looks round him at every jerk of his person forward." The word 'tremendous' has also particular point, for it was, it seems, Dennis' favourite word.

"If," said Gildon, "there is anything of tragedy in the piece (he is referring to Dennis' *Iphigenia*) it lies in the word tremendous, for he is so fond of it he had rather use it in every page than slay his beloved Iphigenia." In the unfortunate farce written in conjunction by Gay and Pope, the *Three Hours after Marriage*, Dennis is introduced as one of the characters and named Sir Tremendous.

588. **tax.** Censure. *Tax* is derived originally from the Latin *tangere*, supine *tactum*, 'to touch,' from whence comes *taxare*, 'to handle,' then 'to reproach' or censure, and lastly 'to rate' or value. So in Shakespeare, *As You Like It*, II. i., "You'll be whipp'd for taxation"—censure or slander. And in this sense 'tax' is used here.

589. **uncensur'd.** See note on line 7.

591. **take Degrees.** Formerly noblemen and the sons of noblemen were admitted to the degree of M.A. in our universities without any examination.

592, 593. **Satires, ... Dedicators.** It is astonishing that Pope could admit such rhymes as these, but see *supra*, 301, 302.

593. **fulsome**, disgusting, properly cloying, satiating; A.-S. for *ful* with the suffix *-sum*.

596. **censure.** See note on l. 7.

599. **rail.** An echo, as Elwin points out, from Buckinghamshire's *Essay on Satire*:

"For who can rail so long as he can sleep."

603. **Jades.** Jade, a sorry nag. Skeat traces it to the Scandinavian *yad* or *yaud*.

606-9 The allusion here is supposed to be to old Wycherley, who, when very advanced in years, went on scribbling bad poetry which Pope, then a mere boy, revised. See Macaulay's amusing account of this in his *Essay on the Comic Dramatists of the Restoration.*

617. **Dryden's Fables ... Durfey's Tales.** Dryden's Fables consist of versions or rather paraphrases of Chaucer's *Knight's Tale*, *Nun's Priest's Tale*, *Wife of Bath's Tale*, *Character of the Good Parson*, and *Flower and Leaf*, with versions of three stories from Boccaccio, and were published not long before his death in 1700. Thomas Durfey, 1653-1723, was a voluminous wit and man of letters of the coarsest order. He was the author of some thirty-one dramatic pieces, and the compiler of six volumes of songs, catches, and the like, called *Pills to Purge Melancholy*. The 'Tales' to which Pope refers are *Tales, Tragical and Comical* (1704), and *Tales, Moral and Comical* (1706). Pope wrote a prologue designed to be spoken at a play acted for Durfey's benefit.

619. **Garth ... Dispensary.** Sir Samuel Garth (1660-1719) was one of the most eminent physicians and wits of his time. Pope had a great liking and respect for him, and in the *Prologue to the Satires* (137) he numbers him among his friends, 'well-natured Garth inflamed with early praise,' referring to the high opinion Dryden had of him, and in his verses on leaving London he says of him:

"The best good Christian he
Although he knows it not,"

referring to Garth's notoriously free opinions on the subject of religion. Dr. Johnson has written his life. The *Dispensary*, a mock heroic poem in six cantos, deals with a then famous feud between the College of Physicians and the Society of Apothecaries. The College passed a resolution to prescribe for the poor and give them medicine gratuitously, and this the apothecaries opposed. The poem was very famous at the time and for a long time afterwards, and it appears from Pope's note that some malignant people attempted to make out that Garth did not write it. It contains one beautiful passage on death, a line from which Cowper incorporated in his poem *On the Receipt of his Mother's Picture*:

"Where billows never break nor tempests roar."

622. **No place so sacred.** Supply 'that' after 'sacred' and 'it' after 'fops.' There are too many of these harsh ellipses in this poem. This stroke of satire is taken literally from Boileau, *Art poétique*, IV. 53-6 (Warton).

623. **Paul's church ... Paul's churchyard.** Pope is referring rather to the reign of Elizabeth, James I., and Charles I., than to his own time. "Then," says Pennant, "the body of St. Paul's Cathedral was the common resort of the politician, the news-monger, and the idle in general. It was called Paul's Walk, and the frequenters of it were known as Paul's Walkers." References to this are common in the Elizabethan writers.

632. **proud to know**, means 'proud of knowing,' *i.e.* of his knowledge; the construction is perfectly legitimate, and is very common in Shakespeare and our old writers. Possibly, however, the passage may mean, still pleased to teach and yet not (too) proud to be taught, to get knowledge; like Chaucer's clerk, "Gladly would he learn and gladly teach."

633. **Unbiass'd.** See note on l. 203.

636. **humanly severe.** "Human and humane are sometimes confounded, though the only authorized sense of the former is *belonging to man*; of the latter, *kind and compassionate.* Humanly is improperly put for humanely in these lines of Pope." *Campbell's Philosophy of Rhetoric*, Bk. II., ch. iii.

642. love to praise. What is meant is a love of bestowing praise: it is the same in construction as the similar idiom in l. 632, though harsher.

645. Stagirite. See note on l. 138.

648. Maeonian Star. Homer. So Horace speaks (*Odes*, I. vi. 2) of a *Maeonium carmen*, a 'Maeonian strain.' Maeonia was an ancient name of Lydia, and Smyrna in Lydia was one of the seven cities which claimed the honour of being Homer's birth-place.

653. Who conquer'd Nature. He is assumed to have 'conquer'd nature' by virtue of being the author of his *Physics*. He presides over wit, in a far more accurate sense, in his *Rhetoric* and *Poetics*. For 'wit' see note on l. 17.

653-60. This is no bad description, roughly speaking, of the style and method of Horace in his *Epistles* and *Ars Poetica*.

662. judge ... phlegm. Phlegm is derived from the Greek φλέγμα, 'flame.' "Phlegm among the ancients signified a cold, viscous humour, contrary to the etymology of the word; but amongst them there were two sorts of phlegm, cold and hot. The use of the word was due to the supposed influence of the four humours, which were: blood, choler, phlegm, and gall, phlegm causing a dull and sluggish temperament" (Skeat, quoting partly from Arbuthnot on *Ailments*). The line is borrowed from Roscommon's essay on translated verse:

"And write with fury, but correct with phlegm."

663, 664. Nor suffers... quotations. How a writer like Pope could allow this couplet to stand is simply inexplicable, it is bad alike in structure, rhythm, and tone. The meaning is the very opposite to what seems to be expressed. What he says is that Horace did not suffer more by wrong translations than critics suffer by wrong quotations. What he plainly means to say is, Horace does not suffer more by the wrong translations of wits, than he does by the misquotations of critics.

665. Dionysius. Dionysius of Halicarnassus, born between B.C. 78 and 54, died B.C. 7. He was a voluminous historian and a voluminous critic. The chief critical writings which have come down to us are some excellent critiques of some of the most eminent Greek orators, and a Treatise on Composition. Pope's eulogy of him is somewhat exaggerated, and indeed not quite intelligible, for in none of his extant works does Dionysius "refine Homer's thoughts," or "call forth new beauties."

667. Petronius. Petronius, surnamed Arbiter, died A.D. 66 by his own hand, is described by Tacitus (*Annals*, XVI. 18, 19) as the most elegant and accomplished voluptuary at the court of Nero. He was the author of a brilliant but shamefully immoral romance called the *Satyricon*, and it is both amazing and ridiculous in Pope to give him a place beside Quintilian and Longinus.

His title to a place among critics begins and ends with a few occasional remarks, towards the commencement and in the fourteenth chapter of his romance, on oratory and poetry.

669. **grave Quintilian.** Marcus Fabius Quintilianus, born about A.D. 40, died about A.D. 118, is the most illustrious of the Roman critics. His great work, *De Institutione Oratoriâ*, or as it is sometimes called, *Institutiones Oratoriæ*, is in twelve books and is an elaborate treatise on the complete education of an orator. The tenth book contains a critical account of the principal Greek and Roman writers. Pope's account of the work is as correct as it is terse.

675. **Thee, bold Longinus.** Dionysius Cassius Longinus was born about 213, probably at Athens, but travelling to Palmyra became acquainted with Zenobia, Queen of Palmyra, who made him her teacher and afterwards her confidential adviser. In A.D. 273, when Aurelian took Palmyra, Longinus was put to death for having incited her to rebel against the Romans. Till 1809, when Weiske published his edition of the *Treatise on the Sublime,* it was universally ascribed to Longinus. But Weiske first showed that there are very weighty (but by no means conclusive) reasons for supposing that Longinus was not the author. The question is still *sub judice,* and there in all likelihood it will for ever remain. In any case this Treatise is the most precious contribution to criticism that has perhaps ever been made. Its influence on criticism in every country in Europe has been enormous; it has been a text-book with most of our best critics, and the only places where it has been neglected are, as might be supposed, the English universities. Pope's apostrophe to Longinus is as noble and eloquent as it is strictly just.

680. **Sublime he draws.** Suggested by Boileau's preface to his translation of Longinus: "Souvent il fait la figure, qu'il enseigne; et en parlant du sublime il est lui-même très sublime."

684. **Arts still follow'd.** Education followed the footsteps of the Romans wherever they settled.

685. **same foes.** The barbarians. Rome was sacked in A.D. 410 by Alaric.

686. **Rome.** Pronounced in and before Pope's time *Room.* Cf. the play on the word in Shakespeare's *King John,* III. i.: "That I have room with Rome to curse awhile." Landor always pronounced it so.

691. **a second deluge.** The sons of the Church—Popes and the Catholic priesthood generally. The whole history of Europe, from the Pontificate of Gregory I. to the Renaissance, justifies and illustrates Pope's epigram, that the monks finished what the Goths began.

693. **Erasmus.** No single man contributed more to the dissemination of learning, culture, and intellectual enlightenment than Desiderius Erasmus (born at Rotterdam in 1467, died at Bâle in 1536), whether we regard his services to theology or to humanity.

696. **drove ... off the stage.** He covered the monks with ridicule and contempt, and gave the death-blow to their effete and tottering system in his *Encomium Moriae*, his *Adagia*, and his *Colloquia*.

697. **Leo's golden days.** The Pontificate of Leo X., from 1513-1521, may be taken as the acme of the Renaissance.

704. **Raphael.** Raphael, born 1483, died 1520, settled at Rome in 1508.

705. **Immortal Vida.** Marco Girolamo Vida, whom Pope exalts to this eminence, was born at Cremona about 1490. Entering the Church he became Apostolical Secretary to Clement VII., and in 1532 was made Bishop of Alba. He died at Alba, Sept. 27th, 1566. His works, all of which are in Latin, consist of odes, modelled on Horace's, an epic poem in six books, called the *Christiad* (1535), a poem on the life of Christ, eclogues, modelled on Virgil's, a poem, in two books, on the growth of silkworms, *Bombyces* (1537), modelled on the *Georgics*, an Art of Poetry (*Poetica*, 1527), in three books; and a mock heroic poem on the game of chess, *Scaccia, Ludus*, a marvellous *tour de force*. Vida is certainly one of the most ingenious and accomplished Latin poets of the Renaissance, and was the most popular, which is possibly to be accounted for by the subjects which he treated, for as a Latin poet he had many rivals and perhaps superiors among his contemporaries. Pope has modelled his game of ombre in the *Rape of the Lock* on the *Scaccia*.

709. **from Latium chas'd.** An allusion to the sack of Rome by the Constable Bourbon in 1527, an event which marks, at all events, approximately, the conclusion of the golden age of the Renaissance in Italy.

714. **Boileau.** Boileau-Despréaux, born November 1st, 1636, died March 13th, 1711, is happily chosen by Pope as representing the Golden Age of the Grand Monarch, as he stands in the same relation to the French literature of that era as Dryden and Pope stand to our own—"the great dictator of the realms of rhyme." His worst works are his *Odes*, his best the *Lutrin*, his *Satires* and *Epistles*, and his *L'Art poétique*. The parallel with Horace cannot be extended to his lyrics. Boileau has himself indicated his relation to Horace in the last part of his *Art poétique*:

> "Pour moi, qui, jusqu'ici nourri dans la satire,
> N'osé encore manier la trompette et la lyre,

Vous me verrez pourtant, dans ce champ glorieux,
Vous animer du moins de la voix et des yeux;
Vous offrir ces leçons que ma muse au Parnasse
Rapporta, jeune encore, du commerce d'Horace."

723. **Such was the Muse.** That Pope should, in coming to England, have passed over Spenser, Shakespeare, Milton, and Dryden, and selected "such small deer" as Sheffield, Roscommon, and Walsh, is partly to be ascribed to his desire to confine himself to criticism; but the omission of Dryden is extraordinary. The muse who proclaimed that Nature's chief masterpiece is writing well was the muse of John Sheffield, Earl of Mulgrave, and subsequently Duke of Buckinghamshire: the line is from his *Essay on Poetry*. When Warton said that "Sheffield's reputation was owing to his rank," and De Quincey that "Pope must have been well aware that, among all the poetic triflers of the day there was not one more ripe for the *Dunciad*," they said what probably most people who have waded through his Grace's poetical works would corroborate. They are literally "so middling, bad were better." The only good thing which Sheffield has left is his epitaph, which is singularly pathetic and powerful:

"Dubius, sed non improbus, vixi,
Incertus morior, sed inturbatus.
Humanum est nescire et errare.
Christum adveneror, Deo confido
Omnipotenti, benevolentissimo.
Ens Entium, miserere mei."

Sheffield was born in 1649, and was the son of Edmund, Earl of Mulgrave. He served in the navy in the second Dutch War, and was one of the few honest courtiers in the service of James II. He filled various important posts; was created in 1703 Duke of Normanby and Duke of Buckinghamshire: he died in Feb. 1720, and has left some memoirs and prose essays which are far more interesting than his poetry.

725. **Roscommon.** Wentworth Dillon, Earl of Roscommon, was born in or about 1633, and was the son of a sister of Strafford. At the Restoration he came to England, and amused himself with various literary projects, among others with founding an English Academy. He died in 1684. His poems consist of *An Essay on Translated Verse*, some short miscellaneous poems, among them a spirited version of the *Dies Irae*, and a translation into blank verse of Horace's *Ars Poetica*. He is a respectable mediocrity, respectable in a double sense, as Pope's couplet indicates:

"In all Charles' days
Roscommon only boasts unspotted lays."
Imit. of First Epist. of First Book of Horace's Epistles.

729. **Walsh.** William Walsh was born about 1663, was educated at Oxford, came up to London and became distinguished as a man of fashion and a wit. Dryden, who was very friendly with him, called him "the best critic in the nation." In or about 1703 he made the acquaintance of Pope, and advised him to aim at 'correctness.' He died in 1708. His poems, which are perfectly mediocre, consist of elegies, epitaphs, odes, and songs, among which is to be found what was a rare phenomenon in the poetry of that day—a sonnet. In the Prologue to the *Satires*, Pope numbers him among his early friends:

"And knowing Walsh would tell me I could write."

Pope's tribute to him here is singularly touching, as it was so perfectly disinterested.

736. **pruned**. The word applied to birds means 'to remove superfluous feathers,' 'to trim their wings'; a variation of the word is 'preen.' 'Tender' in the Latin sense of 'young.'

739, 740. It is remarkable that a well-known quotation often attributed to Horace, "Indocti discant et ament meminisse periti," is a translation of this couplet. It was made by the President Henault, who inserted it as the epigraph to his *Ábrégé chronologique*, not indicating its source. For some time it was attributed to Horace, to the great amusement of Henault, who, however, in the third edition of his work, confessed the hoax. (See Edouard Fournier's *L'Esprit des Autres.*)

INDEX TO THE NOTES.

The first figure denotes the line in the poem, the second the page on which the note will be found.

GLASGOW: PRINTED AT THE UNIVERSITY PRESS BY ROBERT MACLEHOSE AND CO.

GOLDEN TREASURY OF SONGS AND LYRICS. Book Second. By W. BELL, M.A. 3s. 6d.

GRAY—POEMS. By JOHN BRADSHAW, LL.D. 1s. 9d.

Dublin Evening Mail—"The Introduction and Notes are all that can be desired. We believe that this will rightly become the standard school edition of Gray."

Schoolmaster—"One of the best school editions of Gray's poems we have seen."

HELPS—ESSAYS WRITTEN IN THE INTERVALS OF BUSINESS. By F. J. ROWE, M.A., and W. T. WEBB, M.A. 1s. 9d.

The *Literary World*—"These essays are, indeed, too good to be forgotten."

The *Guardian*—"A welcome addition to our school classics. The introduction, though brief, is full of point."

JOHNSON—LIFE OF MILTON. By K. DEIGHTON. 1s. 9d.

LAMB—THE ESSAYS OF ELIA. First Series. Edited by N. L. HALLWARD, M.A., and S. C. HILL, B.A. 3s.; sewed, 2s. 6d.

MACAULAY—ESSAY ON ADDISON. By J. W. HALES, M.A. [*In the Press.*

—ESSAY ON WARREN HASTINGS. Ed. by K. DEIGHTON. 2s. 6d.

—LIFE OF DRYDEN. By P. PETERSON. [*In the Press.*

—LIFE OF POPE. By P. PETERSON. [*In the Press.*

—LORD CLIVE. Edited by K. DEIGHTON. 2s.

—ESSAY ON BOSWELL'S LIFE OF JOHNSON. Edited by R. F. WINCH, M.A. 2s. 6d.

MALORY—MORTE D'ARTHUR. Edited by A. T. MARTIN, M.A. [*In the Press.*

MILTON—PARADISE LOST, BOOKS I. and II. By MICHAEL MACMILLAN, B.A. 1s. 9d. Books I.-IV. separately, 1s. 3d. each; sewed, 1s. each.

The *Times of India*—"The notes of course occupy the editor's chief attention, and form the most valuable part of the volume. They are clear, concise, and to the point, . . . while at the same time they are simple enough for the comprehension of students to whom Milton without annotation must needs be a mystery."

The *Schoolmaster*—"The volume is admirably adapted for use in upper classes of English Schools."

The *Educational News*—"For higher classes there can be no better book for reading, analysis, and grammar, and the issue of these books of Paradise Lost must be regarded as a great inducement to teachers to introduce higher literature into their classes."

—L'ALLEGRO, IL PENSEROSO, LYCIDAS, ARCADES, SONNETS, &C. By WILLIAM BELL, M.A. 1s. 9d.

The *Glasgow Herald*—"A careful study of this book will be as educative as that of any of our best critics on Aeschylus or Sophocles."

—COMUS. By the same. 1s. 3d.; sewed, 1s.

The *Dublin Evening Mail*—"The introduction is well done, and contains much sound criticism."

The *Practical Teacher*—"The notes include everything a student could reasonably desire in the way of the elucidations of the text, and at the same time are presented in so clear and distinct a fashion, that they are likely to attract the reader instead of repelling him."

—SAMSON AGONISTES. By H. M. PERCIVAL, M.A. 2s.; sewed, 1s. 9d.

The *Guardian*—"His notes are always of real literary value. . . . His introduction is equally masterly, and touches all that can be said about the poem."

MACMILLAN AND CO., LIMITED, LONDON.

MILTON—TRACTATE OF EDUCATION. By E. E. MORRIS, M.A. 1s. 9d.

POEMS OF ENGLAND. A Selection of English Patriotic Poetry, with notes by HEREFORD B. GEORGE, M.A., and ARTHUR SIDGWICK, M.A. 2s. 6d.

POPE—ESSAY ON MAN. Epistles I.-IV. Edited by EDWARD E. MORRIS, M.A. 1s. 9d.

—ESSAY ON CRITICISM. Edited by J. C. COLLINS, M.A. [*In the Press.*

SCOTT—THE LADY OF THE LAKE. By G. H. STUART, M.A. 2s. 6d.; sewed, 2s. Canto I., sewed, 9d.

—THE LAY OF THE LAST MINSTREL. By G. H. STUART, M.A., and E. H. ELLIOT, B.A. 2s. Canto I., sewed, 9d. Cantos I.-III., and IV.-VI., 1s. 3d. each; sewed, 1s. each.

The *Journal of Education*—"The text is well printed, and the notes, wherever we have tested them, have proved at once scholarly and simple."

—MARMION. By MICHAEL MACMILLAN, B.A. 3s.; sewed, 2s. 6d.

The *Spectator*—" . . . His introduction is admirable, alike for point and brevity."

The *Indian Daily News*—"The present volume contains the poem in 200 pages, with more than 100 pages of notes, which seem to meet every possible difficulty."

—ROKEBY. By the same. 3s.; sewed, 2s. 6d.

The *Guardian*—"The introduction is excellent, and the notes show much care and research."

SHAKESPEARE—THE TEMPEST. By K. DEIGHTON. 1s. 9d.

The *Guardian*—"Speaking generally of Macmillan's Series we may say that they approach more nearly than any other edition we know to the ideal school Shakespeare. The introductory remarks are not too much burdened with controversial matter; the notes are abundant and to the point, scarcely any difficulty being passed over without some explanation, either by a paraphrase or by etymological and grammatical notes."

—MUCH ADO ABOUT NOTHING. By the same. 2s.

The *Schoolmaster*—"The notes on words and phrases are full and clear."

—A MIDSUMMER-NIGHT'S DREAM. By the same. 1s. 9d.

—THE MERCHANT OF VENICE. By the same. 1s. 9d.

—AS YOU LIKE IT. By the same. 1s. 9d.

—TWELFTH NIGHT. By the same. 1s. 9d.

The *Educational News*—"This is an excellent edition of a good play."

—THE WINTER'S TALE. By the same. 2s.

—KING JOHN. By the same. 1s. 9d.

—RICHARD II. By the same. 1s. 9d.

—HENRY IV., Part I. By the same. 2s. 6d.; sewed, 2s.

—HENRY IV., Part II. By the same. 2s. 6d.; sewed, 2s.

—HENRY V. By the same. 1s. 9d.

—RICHARD III. By C. H. TAWNEY, M.A. 2s. 6d.; sewed, 2s.

The *School Guardian*—"Of Mr. Tawney's work as an annotator we can speak in terms of commendation. His notes are full and always to the point."

—HENRY VIII. By K. DEIGHTON. 1s. 9d.

CPSIA information can be obtained at www.ICGtesting.com
Printed in the USA
LVOW09s1333050916

503268LV00020B/545/P